ADVENTURES IN NEW KENTUCKY COOKING

WITH THE BLUEGRASS PEASANT

DAVID DOMINÉ

10-digit International Standard Book Number 0-913383-97-X
13-digit International Standard Book Number 978-0-913383-97-1
Library of Congress Card Catalog Number 2007930625

Cover design and book layout by Asher Graphics
Divider photographs by Jim Asher
Recipe photographs by David Dominé

Styling for David Dominé provided by Tim Pardue and Studio 101

Manufactured in China

All book order correspondence should be addressed to:

McClanahan Publishing House, Inc.
P.O. Box 100
Kuttawa, KY 42055

McClanahan
Publishing House

270-388-9388
800-544-6959
270-388-6186 FAX

www.kybooks.com

Dedication

For Isabel Zañartu, a precocious two-year-old with a great appetite. She'll make a great food writer some day.

Acknowledgments

I would like to thank previous cookbook authors whose works have proved invaluable in the researching and testing of many of the recipes in this book. To name a few, they are Marion Flexner, Sarah Fritschner, Camille Glenn, Marty Godbey, Cissy Gregg, Irene Hayes, Duncan Hines, Susan Spicer Lowery, Colonel Michael Edward Masters, Elizabeth Ross, Mark Sohn, Michelle Stone and Sharon Thompson. I also owe a huge debt of gratitude to the many cooks, chefs and foodies across the Bluegrass who have shared their stories, secrets and tips with me, and to those who have provided me with encouragement and support. Some of them are: Chuck and Sheelah Anderson, Alan Arnett, Kelly Atkins, Sheila Berman, Gabriele Bosley, Alan and Anne Bird, Judy Cato, Polly Clark, Don Driskell, Ron and Jane Harris, Gene and Norma Johnston, Don and Chris Lowe, Frances Mengel, Jeff Perry, John Reiliford, Jerry Lee Rodgers, Sara Rowan, Scott and Sharon Risinger, Lewis Shuckman, Miss Wanda Stanley, Kent Thompson, Lillie Trimble, Herb and Gayle Warren, and Michael and Rhonda Williams. Thanks to Paula Cunningham, Michelle Stone, Jo Doty and all the others at McClanahan Publishing House who have made this project possible, and to Jim Asher for the design and layout of the book. Finally, a big thanks to all the farmers and artesanal foodmakers in this area of the country that have shaped Bluegrass cuisine.

Special Thanks

I would especially like to thank the many people who graciously offered to taste many of the dishes in this cookbook, and moreover, to test the recipes. They are Michael and Laura Horan, Dick Harrington, Ron and Jane Harris, Jane Newsom, Lynn Shanks, and Silvia Zañartu.

Contents

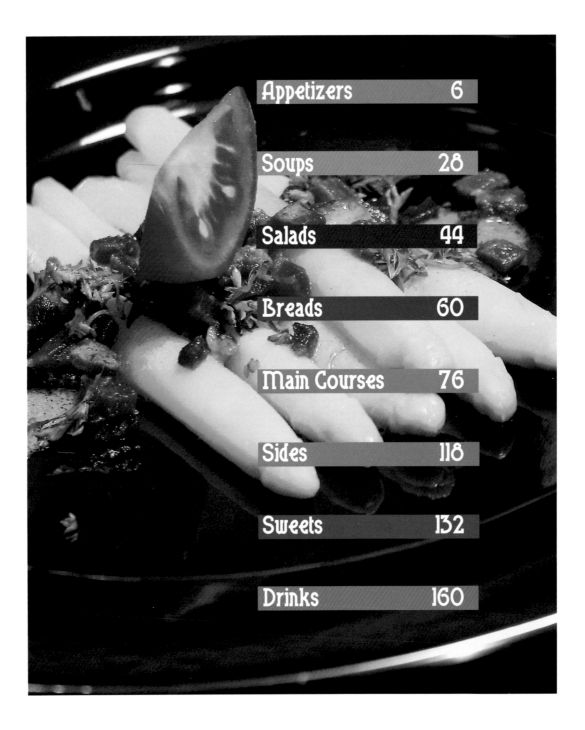

Introduction

Kentucky boasts an enviable culinary history, and no state in the U.S. – with the notable exception of Louisiana – can lay claim to such a remarkable gastronomic identity.

Fine bourbons, country hams and individual flavors associated with the distinctive thoroughbred and tobacco industries form the basis for a rich heritage in the kitchen. Add a healthy dose of pioneer history, native-American and African-American influences, mountainfolk self-reliance and Bluegrass ingenuity, and you've got the makings for a distinctive tradition of cooking and hospitality that makes Kentucky a leader in the domestic arts.

In the western part of the state, where large lakes dot the countryside, fried fish and regional variations on typical southern barbecue have emerged as specialties. In the far reaches of the eastern part of the state, where jagged foothills imprinted the culinary landscape with rugged can-do attitude, staples such as corn, potatoes, pumpkins, nuts, apples, pawpaws and pork combined to create hearty mountain fare that typifies traditional Kentucky cuisine.

Recent gourmet innovations involving locally produced wines, chocolates, prawns and caviars have added a new twist to the epicurean character of the state.

The limestone-rich soil and the rolling countryside of the central district of the state bring all these flavors and influences together in an idyllic area known as the Bluegrass Region. Celebrated for its abundance and southern sense of hospitality, the Bluegrass has come to symbolize all the best Kentucky has to offer, and the lively kitchens in the area showcase local tastes in a multitude of mouthwatering recipes and dishes. The Bluegrass Peasant invites you on a tasty journey along the foodways of this uniquely American state and wishes you many adventures in good eating.

Appetizers

Country Ham Croquettes
Page 9

Green Potato Cakes

Southerners love their greens, and this recipe offers a nice alternative to the standard cooked-in-pot-liquor variety. A satisfying mixture of leftover mashed potatoes and turnip greens (other greens or spinach may also be used) becomes even more appetizing once fried to a deep golden brown. Asiago cheese, rich and nutty, from Kenny Mattingly's farm in Barren County, adds a flavorful zing to this hearty dish.

2 cups cold mashed potatoes
I cup cooked, chopped, well-drained turnip or collard greens
1/4 cup grated Asiago cheese
I teaspoon kosher salt
1/2 teaspoon ground white pepper
1/2 teaspoon freshly grated nutmeg
1/2 cup flour
1/2 cup saffron oil for frying

Combine all ingredients except the flour and olive oil. Using your hands, take a golf-ball-size portion of the mixture and form a cake about 3/4-inches thick. Gently dredge in the flour and fry in the oil that has been heated for five minutes over a medium-low heat. When each side is golden brown, remove the cakes from the hot oil, sprinkle immediately with extra kosher salt and set on a paper towel to absorb the excess oil. Garnish with shavings of Asiago cheese, if desired, and enjoy.

2 cups precooked, finely chopped
    Colonel Newsom's country ham
2 cups fresh bread crumbs
1/4 cup finely chopped dill pickle
3 large eggs
2 tablespoons stone-ground
    mustard
1/2 teaspoon ground black pepper
1/2 teaspoon ground marjoram
1/2 cup flour
1 cup safflower oil for frying
Extra stone-ground mustard
    for dipping

Country Ham Croquettes

Combine the ham, 1 cup of the bread crumbs, pickle, 1 egg, mustard and spices together until well mixed. Using 2-3 tablespoons of the mixture at a time, form small egg-shaped croquettes. Whisk the two remaining eggs together with a tablespoon of water and gently dredge each croquette in flour before dipping in the egg mixture. Shake off the excess egg wash from each croquette and roll in the remaining bread crumbs until well coated. (If possible, chill the croquettes in the refrigerator for an hour or so before proceeding, as this will help them hold together when frying.) Fry in oil that has been heated for five minutes over a medium flame until deep brown. Remove from the hot oil and set on a paper towel to absorb the excess oil. Garnish with slivered spring onions and serve immediately with stone-ground mustard for dipping.

Although any country ham will do, this recipe calls for Colonel Newsom's country ham, a product from Princeton known by connoisseurs and foodies the world over. The curing method, dating to an old family will from the 1770s, involves a combination of time and know-how whereby the hams are hand-rubbed with salt and brown sugar and then hickory smoked.

Pecan Chicken Salad Canapés

Canapés are small hors d'oeuvres meant to be held in the hand and eaten in one or two bites. Usually served atop a piece of bread or cracker, they are often carefully decorated or garnished for special occasions. Because they can often be labor-intensive, they fell out of favor in the convenience-crazed 60s and 70s; however, they remain the classic appetizer for simple get-togethers or elegant cocktail parties.

**4 large boneless, skinless chicken
 breasts, cooked and
 finely chopped
1 cup finely chopped pecans
3/4 cup mayonnaise
2 medium shallots, finely diced
1 tablespoon hot sauce
1 tablespoon bourbon
1 teaspoon salt
1/2 teaspoon ground white pepper
Fresh parsley sprigs for garnish
24 miniature sour milk rolls or
 slices of crusty white bread**

Combine the chopped chicken, pecans, mayonnaise, shallots, bourbon, salt and pepper until well mixed. (If possible, allow to sit in the refrigerator for 2-3 hours until the flavors have blended.) Slice the rolls in half lengthwise and top each piece with 1-2 tablespoons of the chicken salad. Garnish with parsley and serve. Toasted pecan halves may also be used for decoration.

Smoked Spoonfish with Sweet Potato Pancakes

In recent years, some local tobacco farmers have turned to aquaculture with fortunate results for Bluegrass gastronomy. One of the tastiest byproducts has been the spoonfish, also known as the paddlefish or spoonbill catfish, and its firm, white flesh has become a favorite with seafood aficionados across the country. Lewis Shuckman of Louisville, a third-generation meat monger who operates the family business at his Main Street smokery, has parlayed tradition and good taste to produce a wide variety of delicacies that embody the best Kentucky flavors. His smoked spoonfish has gained national recognition for its exceptional quality, and here it provides the perfect accompaniment for savory pancakes flavored with sweet potato.

1 1/2 cups sifted all-purpose flour
2 teaspoons baking powder
2 teaspoons sugar
1 teaspoon salt
1/2 teaspoon freshly grated
   nutmeg
1 1/4 cups cooked mashed
   sweet potato
2 eggs, slightly beaten
1 1/2 cups buttermilk
1/4 cup melted butter
Vegetable oil for frying
1 cup flaked smoked spoonfish
Unsweetened whipped cream and
   chopped green onion for garnish

Sift all the dry ingredients into a mixing bowl. Combine remaining ingredients and add to flour mixture, stirring until moistened. Drop by tablespoons onto a hot greased griddle or skillet and fry, turning once, until browned on both sides. Serve warm with a dollop of whipped cream topped off with flaked spoonfish and green onion.

Sweet Corn and White Hominy Fritters with Spicy Bourbon Sauce

Corn fritters are common sights in country kitchens in many regions of the U.S., but this version incorporates kernels of white hominy and a bourbon-based chile dipping sauce for an extra bit of Bluegrass flavor.

1/2 cup peanut oil for frying
1 cup frozen sweet corn kernels,
   thawed and well drained
1 cup white hominy
1 cup all-purpose flour
3/4 cup buttermilk
1/4 cup sliced green onion
2 cloves garlic, finely chopped
1 large egg, beaten
1 teaspoon kosher salt
1 teaspoon ground white pepper
1/2 teaspoon ground cumin
1/4 teaspoon baking powder

Heat the oil in a large nonstick skillet over medium-high heat. Combine the remaining ingredients to form a thick batter. For each fritter, spoon 1-2 tablespoons of the batter into the pan and fry until golden on both sides. Remove from the oil, sprinkle with salt and drain on paper towels. Garnish with finely sliced green onion and leftover kernels of white hominy and serve with Spicy Bourbon Sauce.

Spicy Bourbon Sauce

1/2 cup chipotle chiles
1/2 cup bourbon
   (W.L. Weller works well here)
1/2 cup cider vinegar
3/4 cup honey
1 1/2 teaspoons kosher salt
1 clove garlic, finely chopped

Combine all the ingredients in a blender and purée until smooth. Transfer the mixture to a saucepan over medium heat and bring to a boil. Reduce the heat and cook for 10 minutes or until the mixture begins to thicken. Remove from heat and cool before serving.

White Cheddar Quiche with Country Ham and Bacon

On a trip to Holland, Kenny Mattingly became inspired to try his hand at cheese making, and in the summer of 1998 he began producing authentic natural gourmet cheeses using milk from hormone-free cows raised on the family farm in Austin. Since then, the repertoire has expanded to include almost 20 varieties of American and European-inspired cheeses. Aged white Cheddar, one of the most popular sorts, combines nicely with Kentucky country ham and bacon for a tasty variation on a quintessential French dish.

1 cup heavy cream
6 large eggs
2 cups grated white
  Cheddar cheese
12 strips of bacon, fried and
  crumbled (about 1 cup)
1 large country ham steak, fried
  until crisp and diced
  (about 1 cup)
2 large shallots, finely chopped
1/4 teaspoon kosher salt
1/4 teaspoon freshly grated
  nutmeg
1/2 teaspoon ground white pepper
9-inch Bluegrass pastry crust

Whisk together the cream and eggs until frothy and pale yellow. Add the remaining ingredients, combining well, and pour into the unbaked pastry crust. Bake in a 350-degree oven for 45 minutes to an hour, or until the egg mixture is firm and the top is golden brown. If desired, an extra 1/4 cup of grated cheese may be sprinkled over the top of the quiche for the last 15 minutes of baking.

Bluegrass Pastry Crust

2 cups sifted all-purpose flour
1 teaspoon salt
1 teaspoon granulated sugar
1/2 cup (1 stick) unsalted butter
1/4 cup lard
1/4 cup chilled bourbon
  (or ice water, if you must)

Combine the flour, salt, sugar and butter and lard, rubbing the mixture together between your hands until it assumes a coarse meal consistency with pea-size lumps. (A food processor may also be used.) Add the egg yolk and mix, adding spoonfuls of the chilled bourbon until the dough starts to come together and pulls away from the sides of the bowl. Turn out onto a floured board and gently kneed the pastry until a soft, smooth dough forms. Be careful not to over kneed, as this tends to yield a tougher crust. Roll out to about 1/4-inch thickness and line the bottom of a deep-dish 9-inch pie pan, making sure to give the edges a decorative crimp.

Smoked Salmon Patties with Bourbon Dill Sauce

For many, salmon patties conjure up flavorless images of boring, post-war American cuisine where frozen dinners and tin cans dominated the culinary landscape. This recipe, however, forgoes the bland canned variety of salmon and calls for a tasty blend of fresh salmon and smoked nova salmon from Shuckman's Fish Company and Smokery in Louisville. A healthy splash of bourbon in the accompanying dill sauce adds a flavorful twist to this comfort-food standard.

3 cups fresh salmon, poached,
   flaked and cooled
1 cup smoked nova salmon,
   chopped
1 cup fresh bread crumbs
1/4 cup mayonnaise
1 large egg, beaten
2 medium shallots, diced
   (about 1/4 cup)
2 tablespoons chopped capers
1 teaspoon kosher salt
1 teaspoon fresh ground
   black pepper
1 cup flour for dredging
1/4 cup canola oil for frying

Poach fresh salmon by placing a large, boneless fillet in a pan of cool, salted water and then heating it over medium heat until bubbles start to form around the edge. Turn off the heat and let sit for 30 minutes. You can also place the pan in a 350-degree oven for 30 minutes, remove and allow to sit for 30 minutes. Remove the fish from the liquid and cool. Use a fork to break apart the salmon and put three cups in a large bowl. Don't worry if the fish hasn't cooked all the way through, since it will be fried anyway. Add the remaining ingredients and gently mix until well incorporated. Chill for 1-2 hours. Portion out equal-size mounds of the fish mixture and shape into round, 1/2-inch patties. Gently dredge in flour and fry in hot oil until golden brown on both sides.

Bourbon Dill Sauce

1 cup sour cream
1/2 cup mayonnaise
3 tablespoons bourbon
2 tablespoons fresh dill, chopped
1/2 teaspoon kosher salt
1 teaspoon ground white pepper

Combine all the ingredients and mix well. Chill for 1 hour and serve with warm salmon patties.

necessitates cleaning. This recipe combines one of Kentucky's newest products – freshwater prawns – with one of its oldest – fine bourbon – to produce a zesty Bluegrass treat.

**18 whole freshwater prawns,
  shells on
1 cup bourbon (I like to use
  Woodford Reserve here.)
Juice of 8 lemons
4 cloves of garlic, crushed
1 teaspoon kosher salt
2 teaspoons cracked black pepper
1/4 cup olive oil
Chopped parsley for garnish**

Grilled Freshwater Prawns with Bourbon and Lemon

One of the tastier results of the recent trend toward diversification away from tobacco farming has been the pursuit of aquaculture in Kentucky. Abandoned coal mines and man-made ponds have become the breeding ground for species of seafood previously unknown to Bluegrass waters, and the state has emerged as a leading producer of *Macrobrachium rosenbergii*, also known as the Malaysian or giant river prawn. They tend to be very easy to prepare since prawns, unlike shrimp, usually do not have a highly visible vein that

Rinse the prawns and place in a large bowl with the bourbon, lemon juice, garlic, salt and pepper. Toss until well coated and marinate in the refrigerator for one hour. Heat a grill or grill pan to medium-high and remove the prawns from the marinade, reserving the liquid in a saucepan placed over high heat. Toss the prawns in the olive oil and place on the grill, cooking about 3-4 minutes on each side. While the prawns grill, stir the cooking marinade until the mixture thickens and reduces by half. Remove the prawns from the heat, arrange on a serving platter and drizzle with the reduction before correcting the seasoning and garnishing with the chopped parsley.

4 cups frozen butter beans or
  baby lima beans
2 cups water
2-3 teaspoons salt
1 teaspoon ground cumin
3 tablespoons fresh lemon juice
3 tablespoons bourbon
6 tablespoons extra-virgin olive oil
6 large cloves of garlic, minced
1/2 teaspoon ground white pepper
1/4 cup chopped fresh flat-leaf
  parsley

Cook beans, 1 teaspoon salt, and water in a covered saucepan about 10 minutes or until beans are tender. (If frozen or fresh beans can't be found, use canned beans and skip the cooking. If dried beans are used, follow cooking directions on the package.) Drain and transfer to a food processor after they have cooled, 15-20 minutes. Add cumin, lemon juice, bourbon, oil, and garlic and purée until smooth. Transfer to a bowl and season with salt and pepper to taste. Mound dip in a large serving bowl, drizzle with extra olive oil and sprinkle with chopped parsley. Garnish with fresh radish slices or banana pepper rings if desired. Serve with toasted slices of sour mash bread.

Butter Bean Hummus

Butter beans make frequent appearances on dinner tables throughout the South, and in the hills of eastern Kentucky they were often cooked to a soft mush and served with corn bread for a satisfying and nutritious meal. This updated recipe yields a garlicky Bluegrass version of the traditional Middle Eastern chick-pea hummus. Although lima beans have a slightly different flavor and color than butter beans, they can be substituted here for a tasty dip that is perfect for parties and get-togethers.

Garlic Grits with Shrimp and Red-Eye Gravy

In a state known for its country hams, red-eye gravy evolved as a natural accompaniment served at breakfast, lunch and dinner in kitchens where thrifty cooks used everything – including leftover coffee – in their preparations. Although different versions abound as to the origins of the red-eye name, it most likely stems from the circle of liquid fat with a slightly reddish cast that forms on the surface when the gravy is reduced. In this take on traditional shrimp and grits, sweet Kentucky prawns and flavorful country ham spice up a hearty coastal low country dish.

2 cups milk
2 cups chicken broth
1 teaspoon kosher salt
1 1/2 cups quick-cooking grits
2 tablespoons apple cider vinegar
1/2 teaspoon ground white pepper
1/2 teaspoon fresh nutmeg
1 tablespoon minced garlic
1/4 cup heavy cream
1 cup grated cheese
   (Try Kenny's Smoked Gouda!)
1/4 cup salted butter
1/4 cup diced country ham
2 tablespoons olive oil
2 pounds shelled freshwater prawns
1 teaspoon cornstarch
2 tablespoons bourbon
1 cup black coffee
Salt to taste
Chopped spring onions and
   radish slices for garnish

Bring milk, broth and salt to a boil in a large saucepan with salt. Stir in grits, reduce the heat to low, and cook until thick, about 5-10 minutes. Stir frequently. Remove from the heat and stir in vinegar, spices, garlic, cream, cheese and butter until melted. In a skillet over medium heat, cook the ham in the olive oil until crisp. Add prawns and sauté 2-3 minutes or until pink. Be careful not to overcook. Remove the prawns from the skillet and keep warm. Increase the heat to high and add the cornstarch, stirring to remove any lumps. Add bourbon and coffee and bring the mixture to a boil. Reduce the heat, add salt to taste and return the prawns to the pan. Spread warm grits onto a large serving platter and top with shrimp and gravy. Sprinkle with chopped green onion and halved radish slices and serve.

1 pound dried black-eyed peas
1/2 cup roughly chopped red onion
2 tablespoons chopped garlic
2 tablespoons chopped parsley
2 tablespoons fresh lemon juice
1 teaspoon kosher salt
1/2 teaspoon ground white pepper
1/4 teaspoon ground cumin
1/2 quart canola oil for frying

Frittered Black-Eyed Peas

One of the few dried legumes that can be cooked without soaking, black-eyed peas, or cowpeas, have been eaten for thousands of years in different parts of the world. African slaves in the U.S. no doubt contributed to their introduction as a staple of southern cuisine. These tasty fritters can be enjoyed on their own or dipped in a variety of sauces.

Wash the peas under cold running water and cook in salted water until tender. (Canned beans may also be used.) Purée in a food processor with the onion, garlic, parsley, lemon juice and spices to form a smooth paste. Let mixture sit, uncovered, in the refrigerator for at least 4 hours to allow flavors to blend. Shape tablespoon-size portions of the mixture into balls or oval quenelles until the mixture has been used up and keep cool. Heat the oil in a 5-quart pot, Dutch oven, or in an electric deep fryer over medium-low heat until a thermometer registers about 350 degrees. Fry the fritters in small batches until golden brown on both sides. Remove with a slotted spoon and drain on paper towels. Lightly salt immediately and serve warm garnished with lemon wedges and chopped flat-leaf parsley. For a tasty dipping sauce, combine 1 cup sour cream with 1/2 cup hot sauce.

**Bluegrass Pastry Crust
(See page 15 for crust.)**
2 cups diced, cooked country ham
**2 cups shredded cheese, such as
Kenny's Farmhouse Havarti**
1 tablespoon chopped parsley
2 tablespoons minced shallots
1/2 teaspoon ground white pepper
1/4 teaspoon ground nutmeg
**1 large egg, beaten with
1 teaspoon milk**

Roll out the pastry to 1/4-inch thickness and cut out 4-inch rounds. Combine ham, cheese, parsley, shallots and spices together. Mound 2-3 tablespoons of the mixture in the center of each pastry round. Moisten the edges with a bit of beaten egg and fold over to seal. Crimp the edges with the tines of a fork or by pinching together the thumb and forefinger of each hand to form a decorative band. Brush each turnover with the remaining egg wash and sprinkle lightly with salt. Bake in a 350-degree oven until golden brown, about 15-20 minutes. These turnovers are even better deep-fried. (Skip the egg wash.)

Country Ham and Cheese Turnovers

Spanish-speakers have their empanadas, Italians have the calzone, Brits have pasties, and Americans enjoy turnovers. These wonderful pastries can come with a variety of sweet or savory fillings, and in the Bluegrass, country ham is a preferred ingredient. Add a bit of cheese from Kentucky dairy farms, and the result is a flavorfully piquant taste treat that can be served any time of the day.

Potato Crisps with Bourbon Smoked Salmon

Old Rip Van Winkle Distillery is home to many of the highest-rated bourbons in the world, and Lewis Shuckman features the ten-year variety in his bourbon-cured smoked-fish products. Hardwoods including hickory and oak staves from old bourbon barrels add extra taste to the hand-sliced smoked nova salmon, which receives eight hours of smoking. Here, the distinctive, bourbon-infused flavor of the fish is paired with the earthy goodness of crispy potato cakes and Moody's Pickle Dip, a Louisville favorite.

2 large russet potatoes, peeled
2 large red potatoes,
   peeled and cooked
2 large shallots, finely chopped
   (about 1/4 cup)
1 teaspoon kosher salt
1/2 teaspoon cracked black pepper
1/4 teaspoon grated nutmeg
2 tablespoons unsalted butter
2 tablespoons canola oil
8 ounces bourbon-style
   smoked nova salmon
Moody's Pickle Dip or your own
Lemon wedges and
   chopped fresh chives for garnish

Grate the raw potato and remove excess moisture. Grate the cooked potato and combine with the raw potato, shallots and spices. Set a large cast-iron skillet over a medium heat and add the butter and oil. Form round, thin cakes using 1-2 tablespoons of the mixture and flatten. Fry the cakes on both sides until golden and crisp. Flatten with a spatula to ensure a thin, crispy cake. Remove the cakes from the pan and set on a paper towel and give each a light sprinkle of salt. To serve, take one potato crisp and place a half-teaspoon dollop of the pickle dip on the surface. Top with a slice of smoked salmon and add another dollop of dip. Cover with another potato crisp and repeat the process two more times to produce a triple-decked stack. Top off with a final dollop of pickle dip and sprinkle with chopped chives. Garnish the plate with lemon wedges and streaks of hot sauce and serve warm.

Pickle Dip

8-ounce package cream cheese,
   softened
1/2 cup finely chopped dill pickle
2 tablespoons lemon juice

Combine the cream cheese, dill pickle and lemon juice and mix well.

Kentucky Fried Green Tomatoes with Cucumber Rémoulade

Of all the summertime dishes in this country, fried green tomatoes hold a special place in the hearts of country cooking fans. In the South, where the long and sultry summers ensure a prodigious supply of unripe tomatoes, it's only natural that they have evolved as a regional specialty. Since the Bluegrass is a state that has one foot in the South and the other in the Midwest, this recipe calls for cornmeal and cracker crumbs to produce a light and crispy breading that pairs well with a cool, creamy sauce made with refreshing cucumber. If you can't find any green tomatoes in your own backyard, make sure to purchase them from a local market selling Kentucky Proud produce.

5-6 medium green tomatoes
1 cup buttermilk
1 cup white cornmeal
1 cup saltine cracker crumbs
1/2 teaspoon ground white pepper
1/4 teaspoon cayenne pepper
1 teaspoon granulated sugar
1 teaspoon kosher salt
Peanut oil for frying

Slice the tomatoes in 1/4-inch slices and lay in a shallow dish with the buttermilk. Let marinate for 1 hour if possible. Combine the cornmeal, cracker crumbs, white pepper and cayenne pepper in a large bowl and set aside. Set a large cast-iron skillet over medium heat and add about 1/2 inch of oil. Remove several tomato slices from the buttermilk and shake off the excess. Sprinkle each side with a pinch of sugar and salt and dredge in the cornmeal-crumb mixture until well coated. (Use your hands to pat on the crumbs and pack together if necessary.) Fry the tomato slices until gold and crispy on each side. Remove from the oil and set on a paper towel to absorb excess grease. Repeat until all the tomato slices have been used. For an attractive individual presentation, drizzle a large white plate with blackstrap molasses and stack two or three slices of fried green tomato in the center. Next to it, place a dollop of cucumber rémoulade that is topped with a halved cherry tomato with a parsley sprig inserted in the top.

Cucumber Rémoulade

1 medium English cucumber,
  peeled and finely chopped
1 cup sour cream
1 cup mayonnaise
2 tablespoons apple cider vinegar
2 tablespoons milk
1/2 teaspoon kosher salt
1/2 teaspoon white pepper

Press out excess moisture from the chopped cucumber using a clean hand towel. Combine the cucumber, sour cream, mayonnaise, apple cider vinegar, milk, salt and pepper in a bowl. Cover and chill before serving.

Smoked Catfish Fritters with Bourbon Rémoulade

This recipe calls for a recently evolved southern delicacy — smoked catfish. Lewis Shuckman uses oak and hickory to impart distinctive character and golden perfection to hand-trimmed fillets from fish farm-raised to his exact specifications. The smoky flavor they impart to the crispy fritters pairs nicely with the smoky notes of the bourbon in the spicy rémoulade dipping sauce.

3 eggs, beaten
1 cup buttermilk
2 tablespoons olive oil
2 teaspoons baking powder
1 teaspoon kosher salt
1/2 teaspoon ground white pepper
1/4 teaspoon cayenne pepper
2 cups all-purpose flour, sifted
2 cups flaked, smoked catfish
1/4 cup finely chopped green onion
Vegetable oil for deep frying

Whisk together eggs, milk, and olive oil. Add baking powder, salt, spices and flour, beating until the batter is smooth. Fold in catfish and onion. Heat oil in a deep fryer or a large, heavy saucepan to 360 degrees on a deep-frying thermometer. Drop heaping spoonfuls of batter into the hot oil, one at a time. When the fritters rise to the surface, roll them over with a slotted spoon to brown evenly. Drain on paper towels, sprinkle lightly with salt and serve with Bourbon Rémoulade.

Bourbon Rémoulade

1/4 cup freshly squeezed lemon juice
1/4 cup bourbon
1 1/2 cups olive oil
1/2 cup chopped green onions
1/4 cup capers in brine
2 tablespoons prepared horseradish
3 tablespoons whole-grain mustard
3 tablespoons prepared yellow mustard
3 tablespoons ketchup
3 tablespoons hot sauce
3 teaspoons chopped fresh parsley
1/2 teaspoon kosher salt

Place all ingredients except the oil in a food processor and process for 30 seconds. Continue processing while the olive oil is slowly drizzled into the mixture and a creamy consistency is achieved. Use immediately or refrigerate the sauce for several days in an airtight container.

Soups

Hot Brown Soup
Pages 44 & 45

I pound black-eyed peas
1-2 quarts chicken or
   vegetable stock
6 cloves of garlic, chopped
I large onion, chopped
I cup finely diced carrots
I cup finely diced celery
2 large bay leaves
2 tablespoons tomato paste
I tablespoon Worcestershire sauce
I tablespoon Tabasco sauce
Salt and freshly ground black
   pepper to taste
Sour cream, red pepper strings
   and chopped green onion garnish

Purée of Black-Eyed Peas

Black-eyed peas are common sights on tables throughout the South, especially on New Year's Day when their semblance to coins is meant to bring prosperity in the coming year. This puréed soup blends old-fashioned tradition with new Kentucky tastes for a satisfying treat any time of year.

Rinse the black-eyed peas and soak, covered, in water 30 minutes, if they are dry. If they are fresh or frozen, skip this step. Drain and add enough stock to cover the beans by 2 inches in a large soup pot and bring to a boil. Turn down the heat to very low, and add the garlic, onion, carrots, celery and bay leaves. Cover and simmer, stirring occasionally, for an hour or until a bean easily squashes against the side of the pot with a wooden spoon. Remove the bay leaves and add the tomato paste, Worcestershire sauce and Tabasco sauce. Use a stick blender to purée the mixture until smooth, or purée the soup in a stand blender in small batches until all the soup has been puréed. Season with salt and pepper and serve garnished with sour cream, red pepper strings and green onion.

3 cups dried butter or lima beans
(4 cups frozen or canned may
also be used)
6 cups chicken or vegetable stock
2 medium red potatoes, diced
and peeled
1 medium onion, chopped
1/2 cup finely diced celery
1 cup diced country ham
2 tablespoons apple cider vinegar
1 tablespoon Worcestershire sauce
1 tablespoon hot sauce
1/2 teaspoon ground white pepper
1/4 teaspoon ground cumin

If using dry beans, soak for 2 hours in
warm water. Drain and add all the ingredients to a large soup pot and bring to
a boil. Cover and simmer over low heat
for 45 minutes or until the beans have
cooked. Correct the seasoning with salt
and additional vinegar if needed. Less
cooking time may be required if canned
or frozen beans are used.

Butter Beans and Country Ham

The humble lima bean – also
known as the Haba bean, Burma
bean, Guffin bean, Hibbert bean,
Java bean, Sieva bean, Madagascar
bean, Civet bean or Sugar bean –
has a common name in the South:
the butter bean. Simmered with
root vegetables and a bit of
savory country ham, the flavorful
and nutritious legume doubles as
a hearty meal or appetizing soup.

1 cup flour
2 eggs
2 cups milk
1/2 teaspoon salt
2 tablespoons olive oil
1 quart clear chicken broth
Chopped fresh chives for garnish

Pancake Soup

Immigrants from southern and central Germany brought this tasty recipe to the Bluegrass in the mid-1800s. It utilizes thin, crepe-like pancakes cut into strips as noodles in a clear broth or consommé. For an elegant Old World dinner, garnish with chopped chives and serve before a main course of roast pork and root vegetables.

Whisk together the flour, eggs, milk, and salt to form a smooth, thin batter and let sit for at least 30 minutes. Grease the bottom of a medium-size skillet very lightly with olive oil and heat to medium. Pour 3-4 tablespoons of batter onto the hot skillet, tilting the pan back and forth to spread out the batter if necessary and ensure thin pancakes. Use a spatula to flip the pancake and cook on the other side. Both sides should be golden brown. Repeat the procedure until all the batter is used and stack one on top of the other when done. Slowly bring the broth to a boil. Cut the stacked crepes into thin strips and place a small mound in a soup plate. Ladle hot broth over the pancake strips and garnish with the fresh chives.

2 cups white wine (try the Vidal
   blanc from Equus Run Vineyards)
1 quart chicken broth
4 cups white hominy
2 cups chopped turnip greens
2 cups diced potato
   (peeled new red works well here)
1 large Vidalia onion, diced
4 large cloves of garlic, smashed
2 tablespoons hot sauce
2 teaspoons kosher salt
1 teaspoon white pepper
1 pound pork sausage
1/4 cup all-purpose flour
2 cups milk

White Hominy Stew with Turnip Greens and Country Sausage

Pour the wine and broth in a large stock pot and add all the ingredients except the sausage, flour and milk and bring to a boil. Reduce the heat and simmer. Fry the sausage in a large skillet over medium heat, breaking it apart into quarter-sized pieces as it cooks, and drain off excess fat. Add sausage to simmering stew and cook for 30 minutes more. Whisk the flour into the milk to make a slurry and add to hot soup after turning up the heat. After the stew has thickened slightly, remove from heat and correct the seasonings. Can be served over steamed white rice or with warm corn bread. Add a splash of cider vinegar for an extra bit of flavor.

Reminiscent of a Tuscan white bean and kale soup, this recipe calls for Grandma Broadbent's Smoked Country Pork Sausage, a Trigg County favorite. However, any country-style pork sausage from Kentucky will impart the same satisfying flavor that enhances the earthy goodness of hominy and turnip greens.

Tomato Broth with Goat Cheese Dumplings

Although the Bluegrass hasn't yet developed a strong tradition in the making of goat cheese, Larry and Judy Schad – transplants from the Louisville suburbs – have mastered this art at their Kentuckiana cheeserie in Greenville, Indiana. Their award-winning *chèvre* or goat cheese features nicely in savory dumplings that spice up a delicate tomato broth.

2 tablespoons extra-virgin olive oil
1 large white onion, diced
2 cloves of garlic, minced
1/2 cup diced celery
4 cups chopped Roma tomatoes
2 large bay leaves
1 tablespoon kosher salt
1 teaspoon ground white pepper
6 cups chicken stock
1 cup dry white wine
  (I like Wildside Vines
   Chardonnay)

In a large stockpot, heat the olive oil over medium heat and sauté the onion, garlic and celery until translucent. Add the tomatoes, bay leaves, seasonings, chicken stock and wine and bring to a boil. Reduce the heat and simmer for 30 minutes. Purée the mixture and strain through a sieve, returning the liquid to the pot over medium heat.

Goat Cheese Dumplings

2 cups all-purpose flour
1 teaspoon baking powder
1 teaspoon kosher salt
1/2 teaspoon grated nutmeg
1/2 teaspoon white pepper
2 large eggs, beaten
1 cup Capriole Farms fresh
  goat cheese
1 tablespoon olive oil
Freshly chopped tarragon
  for garnish

Combine the flour, baking powder, salt, nutmeg and pepper in a large bowl. Add the beaten eggs, cheese and olive oil and mix well to form a smooth dough or batter. If necessary, add a few teaspoons of water if the dough is too dry. Turn up the heat and bring the tomato broth to a gentle boil. Drop 1/4-teaspoon size bits of the dough into the boiling liquid and cook for 4-5 minutes. Turn off the heat and let rest for 5 minutes. Correct the seasonings. Ladle broth and dumplings into soup plates or bowls and garnish with chopped tarragon.

White Sweet Potato Bisque

A good source of fiber, complex carbohydrates, and vitamins A and C, Kentucky sweet potatoes can have a dry or moist flesh that ranges from bright orange to pale yellow or white in color. The lightest variety works especially well in this elegant soup flavored with bourbon and ginger.

4 tablespoons unsalted butter
1 large Vidalia onion,
  coarsely chopped
1/2 cup diced carrot
1/2 cup diced celery
2 large cloves of garlic, chopped
2 pounds (about 4 cups) sweet
  potatoes, peeled and diced
5 cups vegetable or chicken stock
2 large bay leaves
1 teaspoon grated fresh ginger
2 teaspoons kosher salt
1 teaspoon white pepper
1 teaspoon curry powder
1/2 cup bourbon
1 cup heavy cream
Crème fraîche for garnish
Chopped chives for garnish

Melt the butter in a large soup pot over medium heat. Add the onion, carrot, celery and garlic and cook 5 minutes or until the onion is translucent. Add the sweet potato and cook for 5 minutes. Turn up the heat and add the stock, bay leaves, ginger, salt, pepper, curry powder and bourbon before bringing to a rolling boil. Lower the heat and simmer for about an hour or until the potatoes are done. Remove the bay leaves and purée the soup using either a hand-held stick blender or a stand blender. Add the heavy cream and return to very low heat. Adjust the seasoning by adding salt, pepper and bourbon to taste. Serve garnished with a dollop of crème fraîche and a sprinkle of chopped chives.

2 tablespoons olive oil
1 large white onion, chopped
1/2 cup diced celery
1/4 cup diced sweet red pepper
2 large cloves of garlic, chopped
2 large bay leaves
5 cups chicken broth
1 bottle Bluegrass Brewing
   Company American Pale Ale
2 teaspoons kosher salt
1 teaspoon ground black pepper
4 cups dried black beans
Hot sauce for garnish
Torn green onion for garnish

Rinse the black beans and soak in warm water for 4-6 hours. In a large stock pot, heat the olive oil over medium-high heat and sauté the chopped onion, celery, pepper and garlic for 3-4 minutes. Drain the black beans and add to the pot, along with the broth, beer, bay leaves and seasonings. Bring to a boil. Reduce the heat and simmer, covered, for 1 hour or until the beans are very tender. Correct the seasoning and serve garnished with hot sauce and torn green onion.

Kentucky Black Bean Soup

Many people associate black bean soup with the cuisine of Spanish-speaking countries in the Caribbean, however, American recipes for this simple, earthy concoction go back for generations. This formula is based loosely on a Kentucky family recipe that dates to the Civil War. The addition of locally brewed pale ale adds a distinctive touch of the Bluegrass to a hearty dish that pairs nicely with a green salad to make a light and tasty meal any time of the year.

Crawfish and Corn Chowder

The most accepted etymology for this quintessential American soup comes from the French word *chaudière,* which means "a pot." Derived from *chaud* or "hot," the word "chowder" is a New England word that arose in Newfoundland, where Breton fishermen would throw portions of the day's catch into a large pot with other available foods. In many parts of the American South, where corn and crawfish could readily be found, this Yankee specialty has been adapted to incorporate regional flavor in a hearty soup.

I large onion, finely chopped
1/2 cup finely chopped celery
2 cloves of garlic, minced
1/2 cup diced country ham
4 tablespoons butter
4 tablespoons flour
2 cups diced potato
4 cups fresh or frozen corn
4 cups seafood or chicken stock
I cup semidry white wine (try the
  Kentucky Chardonnay from
  Lost Heritage Vineyards)
2 tablespoons hot sauce
2 teaspoons kosher salt
I teaspoon ground white pepper
1/2 teaspoon grated nutmeg
1/4 cup chopped flat-leaf parsley
I pound cooked crawfish tails
2 cups heavy cream
Chopped scallions for garnish
Extra hot sauce for garnish

Sauté onion, celery, garlic and ham in butter over medium heat until soft. Whisk in flour, stirring until well blended. Add potatoes, corn, stock, wine, hot sauce, salt, pepper and nutmeg and stir until soup comes to a soft boil. Lower the heat and simmer for 45 minutes to an hour. Add parsley, crawfish tails and cream and simmer for 5 minutes. Correct the seasoning by adding salt and pepper to taste. Garnish each serving with chopped scallion and hot sauce.

8 strips of smoked bacon, diced
2 tablespoons all-purpose flour
2 cups white wine
  (try the Ensemble from
  Chrisman Mill Vineyards)
4 cups potatoes, peeled and diced
3 medium yellow onions,
  coarsely chopped
4 cloves of garlic, chopped
3 cups tomatoes, peeled and diced
6 cups chicken stock
2 cups tomato sauce
1 teaspoon kosher salt
1 teaspoon ground black pepper
3 pounds skinned catfish fillets,
  cut into 1-inch pieces
2 bay leaves
Slivered green onion for garnish

Catfish Muddle

This tomato-and-fish-based soup has its American origins in the chunky chowders of Manhattan and the pine bark stews of the coastal South, where it also came to be known as Carolina bouillabaisse or Carolina muddle. This Kentucky version features smoked bacon and farm-raised catfish to produce a down-home take on a hearty classic.

In a stew pot over medium heat, cook the bacon until crispy. Drain away all but 3 tablespoons of the fat and add the flour, stirring to remove any lumps. Cook over low heat for 4-5 minutes or until the flour turns golden brown. Add the white wine and whisk together as the mixture cooks and thickens. Add potatoes, onions, garlic, tomatoes, stock, tomato sauce, salt, pepper and bay leaves and bring to a boil. Cover and simmer for 1 hour over low heat. Add fish and simmer over very low heat for 30 minutes more. Make sure not to stir too much, as this will break up the fish pieces. Garnish with slivered green onions and serve with warm corn bread or over steamed white rice.

Bluegrass Burgoo

This hearty soup hearkens back to pioneer days when Kentuckians would utilize huge cast-iron kettles and an abundance of local game to satisfy hungry crowds. Although traditional recipes call for at least 24 hours cooking time, this updated, lighter version can be enjoyed in a fraction of the time.

1 large red onion, diced
1 stalk celery, diced
4 cloves of garlic, minced
1 small green bell pepper, diced
2 tablespoons olive oil
1/2 pound diced beef
1/2 pound diced pork
1/2 pound boneless chicken breast, diced
1 cup bourbon
6 cups chicken stock
6 cups beef stock
1/4 cup Worcestershire sauce
2 large potatoes, diced
2 large carrots, diced
1/2 cup lima beans
1/2 cup yellow corn
2 bay leaves
1/2 cup tomato paste
1 tablespoon kosher salt
Fresh ground black pepper to taste
Chopped parsley for garnish

In a large Dutch oven, sauté the onion, celery, garlic and pepper in the olive oil over medium heat. Add the beef, pork and chicken and brown for 2-3 minutes. Add the bourbon and stir to deglaze the bottom of the pan. Add all the remaining ingredients except the tomato paste and bring to a rolling boil. Reduce the heat and simmer, uncovered, for two hours. Stir in tomato paste and salt and pepper to taste before serving. Garnish with fresh chopped parsley.

2 pounds carrots, peeled and diced
1 large yellow onion, chopped
4 large cloves of garlic, smashed
1/4 cup olive oil
1 tablespoon kosher salt
1 teaspoon ground white pepper
1/2 teaspoon thyme
1/2 teaspoon ground ginger
1/2 teaspoon ground cumin
2 bay leaves
1 cup bourbon
5 cups chicken stock
1 cup heavy cream
Fresh nutmeg for garnish
Chopped chives for garnish

Carrot Bourbon Potage

In a large pot or Dutch oven, sauté the carrots, onion and garlic in the olive oil over medium heat until onion turns translucent. Turn up the heat and add the spices and bourbon and cook until the bourbon reduces by half. Return to low heat, add chicken stock and simmer for 30 minutes or until the carrots are tender. Remove the bay leaf and discard. Turn down the heat and use a hand-held blender to purée the soup until completely smooth and free of lumps. Add cream and heat for another 5 minutes, then correct the seasonings and serve. Garnish with fresh grated nutmeg and chopped chives.

Not to be confused with *Pottage*, an English stew-like soup of vegetables and sometimes meat, *Potage* refers to a thick, rich soup – often creamy – made in the traditional French style. Early French settlers in the Bluegrass no doubt used a wide variety of local produce to carry on their soup-making tradition, and this recipe has its origins in the regions of northern France that were renowned for their root vegetables.

Hot Brown Soup

When Chef Fred K. Schmidt used a holiday standard to construct a special sandwich to satisfy the appetites of late-night dancers in Louisville's elegant Brown Hotel in 1926, he probably never imagined that the comforting flavors of turkey, bacon and cheese would one day evolve into a rich and hearty soup. This recipe combines the stars of a Kentucky classic in a new Bluegrass favorite.

8 strips smoked bacon
1 cup finely chopped onion
1/2 cup finely chopped celery
4 large cloves of garlic, minced
2 medium red potatoes, peeled
    and cut in 1/4-inch pieces
3 cups diced turkey breast
2 cups dry white wine
2 cups chicken stock
5 cups milk
2 teaspoons kosher salt
1 teaspoon ground white pepper
1/4 teaspoon ground nutmeg
2 cups heavy cream
1/2 cup all-purpose flour
2 cups shredded aged
    white Cheddar from
    Kenny's Farmhouse Cheeses
Crumbled bacon, chopped tomato,
    and chopped fresh parsley
    for garnish

In a Dutch oven over medium heat, cook bacon until slightly crispy. Add onion, celery and garlic and sauté until tender. Add diced potatoes and turkey and cook, stirring occasionally, until turkey is seared on all sides. Add the wine, turn up the heat and stir to deglaze the bottom of the pan. Cook for 5 minutes and then add the stock, milk, salt, pepper and nutmeg. Simmer over low heat for 15 minutes, or until the potatoes are tender, stirring often to avoid sticking on the bottom. In a small bowl, whisk together cream and flour to make a slurry free of lumps and stir into the simmering soup. After the mixture has thickened, turn off the heat, add cheese and stir. Adjust the seasoning if necessary and serve with slices of toast and desired toppings.

Bluegrass Bouillabaisse

The traditional fisherman's stew based on local fish and shellfish known as bouillabaisse has its origins in the French port city of Marseilles, and today countless variations on the classic Mediterranean dish abound. This Kentuckyfied version incorporates local seafood and produce in a satisfying favorite that is perfect for celebratory get-togethers or simple family dinners.

2 tablespoons extra-virgin olive oil
2 large tomatoes, peeled
  and coarsely chopped
1 large onion, chopped
4 cloves of garlic, chopped
4 cups peeled, diced
  new red potatoes
1 cup fresh or frozen sweet corn
1 cup frozen baby lima beans,
  thawed
1 cup white hominy
2 bay leaves
1/4 teaspoon crumbled saffron
  threads
1 1/2 tablespoons coarse sea salt
1/2 teaspoon black pepper
6 cups chicken stock
3 cups dry white wine
1 pound whole red-claw crayfish
1 pound freshwater prawns
1 pound crayfish tail meat
1 pound boneless, skinless
  catfish filets
Fresh tarragon and lemon peel
  for garnish

Heat oil in a 6- to 8-quart pot over moderate heat. Add tomatoes, onion, and garlic and cook, stirring occasionally, until onion is translucent. Add potatoes, corn, limas, hominy, bay leaves, saffron, sea salt, and pepper. Add stock and wine and bring to a boil. Reduce the heat and simmer, covered, for about 10 minutes or until potatoes are almost tender. Add crayfish, prawns and fish and simmer, uncovered, for about 5 minutes or until they are cooked through. Correct the seasoning, garnish with shredded tarragon and strips of lemon peel and serve with toasted slices of crusty white bread. For an extra touch of the Bluegrass, top off each serving with a generous splash of bourbon.

Salads

2 tablespoons extra-virgin olive oil
1 tablespoon fresh lemon juice
1 teaspoon Dijon mustard
1 teaspoon kosher salt
1 medium shallot, finely chopped
1 green apple, cored and
   thinly sliced
4 small radishes, thinly sliced
4 cups washed, packed spinach
12 ounces flaked,
   boneless Smoked Kentucky Trout

Spinach and Smoked Kentucky Trout

Lewis Shuckman uses Black Mountain trout raised in the cool waters of abandoned coalmines in eastern Kentucky for his three varieties of smoked rainbow trout. Hickory wood and bourbon barrel staves impart the bourbon style with a buttery, mellow flavor that pairs nicely with the snappy bite of fresh spinach.

In a large bowl whisk together oil, lemon juice, mustard and salt. Add shallots, apple, radishes and spinach that has been dried well, tossing to coat. Add flaked trout, tossing to combine. Season with additional salt and pepper to taste.

4 large beets
3 cups Silver Queen corn kernels
  (fresh or frozen, thawed)
1 tablespoon fresh lemon juice
1 tablespoon apple cider vinegar
1/2 teaspoon kosher salt
1/2 teaspoon white pepper
1 tablespoon olive oil
1 tablespoon balsamic vinegar
Bibb lettuce leaves
8 ounces fresh Capriole Farms goat
  cheese, crumbled
Cracked black pepper

Silver Queen Corn with Roast Beets and Goat Cheese

Scrub and wash the beets and place them in a baking dish. Bake in a preheated 400-degree oven for 45 minutes or until the skin has charred slightly and the flesh can be easily pierced with a fork. Remove from the oven and plunge the roasted beets in a large bowl of ice and water. As the beets cool, toss the corn kernels with the lemon juice and cider vinegar, half the salt and pepper, and let sit. Remove the beets from the ice water and remove the skin, which should peel away with ease. Cut each of the beets in eight segments or a large dice and toss together in a large bowl with the olive oil, balsamic vinegar and remaining salt and pepper. To assemble the salad, lay leaves of Bibb lettuce out on a large plate and top with beets and the corn mixture. Dot with goat cheese crumbles and season with fresh cracked black pepper.

Since the hybrid was introduced in 1955, Silver Queen has reigned as one of the best-loved breeds of sweet corn in the southeastern U.S. Although newer varieties are slowly eclipsing the popularity of this breed's tender, pearl-like kernels, Silver Queen remains a summer favorite in Bluegrass kitchens.

Bluegrass Salad

Bibb Lettuce, also called Boston or limestone lettuce, has soft and buttery leaves of a pale green color loosely bunched in small, round heads. The limestone-rich waters of the Bluegrass have made this one of the choicest lettuce varieties in the state, and this fresh salad combines crisp greens with other Kentucky staples like country ham, pecans and bourbon for a fresh and flavorful creation.

1/2 cup corn oil
1/2 cup saffron oil
1/2 cup apple cider vinegar
2 tablespoons balsamic vinegar
2 tablespoons bourbon
4 tablespoons honey
1 teaspoon salt
1/2 teaspoon cracked black pepper

Combine oils, vinegars, bourbon, honey and seasonings in a jar with a tight-fitting lid. Cover tightly, shake to mix well and chill 2 hours before serving.

2 heads Bibb lettuce
1 cup fresh corn kernels
1 medium red onion, thinly sliced
1 pear, thinly sliced
1 cup toasted pecans
1 cup crumbled goat cheese
1 cup country ham crumbles

Combine all the ingredients, toss well with desired amount of dressing and correct the seasonings. If desired, you may reserve some of the pecans and ham and cheese crumbles for the top. To ensure that the red onion slices are sweet instead of strong and pungent, soak them in a container of ice water for 1 hour before incorporating in the salad.

8 large new red potatoes
1/2 cup capers, drained
1/4 cup olive oil
1 cup mayonnaise
1/2 cup sour cream
3 tablespoons apple cider vinegar
3 tablespoons prepared mustard
2 tablespoons prepared horseradish
1 teaspoon kosher salt
1 teaspoon ground white pepper

Southern Potato Salad with Capers

Cook the potatoes in salted, boiling water for 15 minutes. Turn off the heat, and allow the potatoes to sit for another 10 minutes in the hot water. Remove from the pot and plunge the potatoes in cold water for 10 minutes or until cool enough to handle. Peel potatoes and dice into 1/4-inch cubes. Whisk together the remaining ingredients and pour over the diced potatoes, tossing to coat. Allow to chill in the refrigerator for at least 2 hours (the longer, the better) before serving. Adjust the flavor by adding extra ingredients as needed and enjoy. Garnish with minced parsley and chives.

As with apple pie and meat loaf, countless recipes and varieties abound, and everyone claims to have the perfect recipe for potato salad. This formula relies on a simple blend of firm-fleshed potatoes in creamy dressing seasoned with horseradish and an old-fashioned favorite, capers.

Bourbon Caesar Salad with White Cheddar Crisps

Bourbon in the dressing and extra bourbon for the crunchy croutons made from toasted sour mash bourbon bread add a zesty zip to this classic salad. Crispy cheese thins made from Kenny's Farmhouse white Cheddar round out the recipe with a creamy tang.

2 large cloves of garlic, crushed
3-4 anchovy filets
2 tablespoons Dijon mustard
1 teaspoon Worcestershire sauce
1 teaspoon hot sauce
2 tablespoons bourbon
1 tablespoon fresh lemon juice
1 egg
1 teaspoon kosher salt
1/2 teaspoon freshly ground
    black pepper
1/4 cup extra-virgin olive oil
1 small Distiller's Baguette
    (See page 73),
    cut into 1/2-inch cubes
    (about 2 cups)
2 tablespoons melted butter
2 tablespoons bourbon
1/2 teaspoon kosher salt
2 cups finely grated sharp
    white Cheddar cheese
1 large head romaine lettuce,
    rinsed, dried, and torn into
    bite-size pieces
Radishes for garnish

Preheat oven to 300 degrees. Prepare the dressing by using the tines of a fork to mash together the garlic and anchovy filets in a large bowl. Add the mustard, Worcestershire sauce, hot sauce, bourbon and lemon juice and mix well. Use a whisk to mix in the egg, salt and pepper. (If you don't want to use raw egg, coddle it beforehand.) While whisking, slowly pour a thin stream of the olive oil into the mixture to finish the dressing. Prepare the croutons by combining the bread cubes, melted butter, bourbon and salt and toss to coat. Place in a single layer on a baking sheet and put in a preheated oven for 20 minutes. Make cheese crisps by mounding 1/4-cup portions of the grated cheese on a parchment-lined baking sheet and baking in the 300-degree oven for 15 minutes or until the mounds have flattened and turned golden brown. Remove from the oven, and allow to sit for a minute before using a spatula to transfer to a baking rack so they can cool and crisp up. To make the salad, add the romaine to the bowl with the dressing and toss. Immediately prior to serving, add croutons and toss well. Adjust the seasoning, garnish with radish wedges and serve topped with cheese crisps.

Bibb Salad with Bourbon Citrus Vinaigrette

First cultivated by Frankfort horticulturist John Bibb in the mid-1800s, this crisp, buttery variety thrived in the limestone-rich soil of the Bluegrass and soon came to represent the bounty of Kentucky farms. Dressed with bourbon-spiked vinaigrette, it makes the perfect light summertime salad.

2 heads **Bibb lettuce**
1/4 cup **bourbon**
2 tablespoons **Dijon mustard**
2 medium **shallots, chopped**
2 tablespoons **fresh lemon juice**
2 tablespoons **fresh orange juice**
2 tablespoons **honey**
1/2 teaspoon **kosher salt**
1/4 cup **extra-virgin olive oil**
2 small **shallots, sliced, for garnish**

Clean the lettuce leaves and arrange on a large platter. Purée the bourbon, mustard, chopped shallots, juices, honey and salt in a blender until smooth. Slowly drizzle in the olive oil until the dressing has emulsified slightly. Drizzle lettuce with the vinaigrette and garnish with thin slices of shallot and enjoy.

2 tablespoons Dijon mustard
2 large shallots, chopped fine
3 tablespoons apple cider vinegar
3 tablespoons extra-virgin olive oil
3 cups chopped, washed
   turnip greens
2 cups washed mixed salad greens
1 cup very finely chopped
   country ham
1/2 teaspoon kosher salt
1/2 teaspoon freshly ground
   black pepper

Fresh Turnip Greens with Country Ham Vinaigrette

Prepare the dressing by first mixing the mustard and chopped shallots and then whisking in the vinegar and olive oil. Add the greens and ham, toss until well coated and season with salt and pepper to taste. For an extra treat, toast cubes of corn bread in butter and olive oil to make crunchy croutons. If desired, garnish with strips of sweet red pepper.

People who know about southern cooking know that the prime time for turnip greens comes in the fall after a nip from Jack Frost, when these hearty greens rich in calcium and vitamins A and C take on a unique, robust flavor all their own. Although these sturdy, green leaves usually end up cooked in *pot likker*, the younger stalks make an excellent salad. Turnip greens easily fall into that category of foods where many assume they don't like them without even giving them a try. This recipe will change their minds.

2 large English cucumbers, washed
1/4 cup bourbon
1/4 cup Champagne
1/4 cup olive oil
1 teaspoon fresh dill, chopped
1/4 cup finely chopped parsley
2 large shallots, finely chopped
1/4 cup finely diced sweet
   red pepper
1/4 cup apple cider vinegar
1/2 teaspoon kosher salt
1/2 teaspoon cracked black pepper
1/4 cup Champagne

Cucumbers with Bourbon Champagne Mignonette

Mignonette is a thin, shallot-and-vinegar-based sauce often used to accent fish and seafood, especially raw oysters. This Bluegrass adaptation of a favorite late summer salad combines the refreshing elegance of Champagne with the sweet notes of bourbon. The result is crisp cucumber slices spiked with a tart and tangy mignonette that will dress up any picnic table.

Thinly slice cucumbers and set aside. In a small saucepan, bring the bourbon and 1/4 cup Champagne to a low boil and reduce by half. Remove from the heat and let cool. Whisk in the oil, dill, parsley, shallots and red pepper. Add the vinegar, salt and pepper, pour over the cucumbers and mix well. Refrigerate for 2 hours and serve after correcting the seasoning and adding a splash of Champagne.

4 cups Shoe Peg corn
1/2 cup sliced green onion
1/2 cup diced red pepper
1/4 cup olive oil
2 tablespoons apple cider vinegar
1/2 teaspoon kosher salt
1/2 teaspoon ground white pepper

Combine all the ingredients together and refrigerate for 2 hours. Check the seasoning and serve. Warmed, this also makes an excellent side dish.

Shoe Peg Corn Salad

Valued for its sweetness, white Shoe Peg corn is particularly popular in the southern states. The unique name comes from the small, narrow kernels in uneven rows on the cob that resemble the wooden pegs that shoemakers used to attach soles to the upper parts of the shoes in the 1800s. This simple salad can be made with fresh, frozen or canned kernels and makes a perfect side or salad dish any time of year.

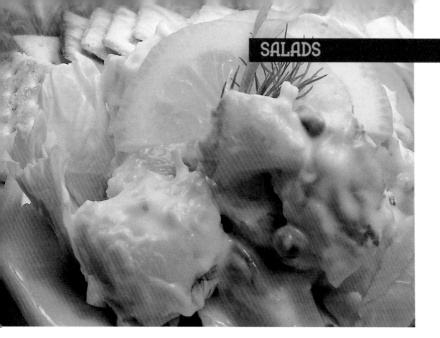

Kentucky Lobster Salad

Aside from caviar and shrimp, Kentucky has also made gains in the cultivation of another gourmet seafood item, lobster. Although some sticklers might point out that the succulent meat of the *Kentucky lobster* is actually that of the large red-claw crayfish, it is just as sweet and tasty as that of its Maine cousin. In a salad with a light dressing of lemon juice and mayonnaise, it can be served by itself on a crisp bed of Kentucky Bibb lettuce or atop split sour mash rolls for a tasty Kentucky treat.

4 cups red-claw crayfish, cooked and chopped
2 tablespoons fresh lemon juice
2 tablespoons white wine vinegar
1/4 cup mayonnaise
1 tablespoon chopped capers
1 tablespoon fresh tarragon
1 small shallot, minced
1/2 teaspoon sea salt
1/2 teaspoon ground white pepper
1 small head Bibb lettuce

Lightly toss the crayfish with the lemon juice and vinegar. Add the mayonnaise, capers, tarragon, shallot, salt and pepper and mix until moistened. Chill for two hours in the refrigerator and serve atop a bed of the Bibb lettuce.

1 small English cucumber
1/2 white or yellow onion
1/4 cup chopped parsley
1/4 cup olive oil
1/2 cup softened cream cheese
1/2 cup sour cream
1/4 cup mayonnaise
1/4 cup apple cider vinegar
1/2 teaspoon kosher salt
1/2 teaspoon white pepper
2 heads Bibb lettuce

Grate the cucumber (skin and all) and the onion by hand or with a food processor. Place the grated vegetables in the center of a clean dishtowel, draw up the ends and squeeze out all the excess moisture. (You should be able to extract at least half a cup of liquid.) Make the dressing in a blender by first puréeing the parsley and olive oil until smooth. Add the remaining ingredients, except the lettuce, and blend well. Arrange cleaned lettuce leaves on a large platter and drizzle with the benedictine dressing. May be garnished with salted tomato wedges and chopped, toasted pecans if desired.

Butter Lettuce with Benedictine Dressing

Bibb lettuce is commonly referred to as *butter lettuce* in Kentucky because of its creamy texture and velvety leaves. This salad pairs the delicate leaves of Bluegrass lettuce with an appropriately creamy dressing based on the cucumber spread made famous by Louisville caterer, Jennie Benedict, in the 1800s.

1 small head green cabbage
2 large carrots, scrubbed
1 small yellow onion
2 tablespoons Dijon mustard
1 tablespoon honey
1/4 cup bourbon
1/4 cup apple cider vinegar
1 teaspoon kosher salt
1 teaspoon freshly ground
  black pepper
2 cups crumbled Kenny's
  Farmhouse Kentucky
  Bleu Cheese
1/2 cup chopped flat-leaf parsley
Radish slices for garnish

Bourbon Bleu Cheese Slaw

Although coleslaw has become an integral part of the American culinary landscape, especially in the South where it often appears alongside barbecue and other summertime favorites, its roots go back many centuries. Most agree that the name arises from the Dutch word for *cabbage salad* and that European settlers brought it to this country, however, all you need to do is add a good splash of bourbon and some tangy bleu cheese from a Kentucky farmer to make it a true specialty from the Bluegrass.

Cut the cabbage in half and then in quarters after cutting out the core. Use a food processor to julienne the cabbage, carrots and onion and transfer into a large bowl, discarding any large pieces. You should have about 8 cups. In a medium bowl, whisk together the mustard, honey, bourbon, vinegar, salt, and pepper. Pour dressing over the grated vegetables to toss and moisten. Add crumbled bleu cheese and parsley and combine. Cover the bowl and refrigerate for 30 minutes to allow the flavors to blend. Serve cold or at room temperature. Garnish with sliced radish halves for an extra zing.

6 large sweet potatoes
12 strips of smoked bacon
1 medium red onion, thinly sliced
3 tablespoons whole-grain mustard
3 tablespoons apple cider vinegar
3 tablespoons balsamic vinegar
2 tablespoons honey
1 teaspoon kosher salt
1/2 teaspoon cracked black pepper
Chopped parsley

Bake the sweet potatoes in a 400-degree oven for 30 minutes or until the flesh can be easily pierced. While the potatoes bake, heat a skillet over medium heat and fry the bacon strips until slightly crisp. Remove the strips from the pan, drain and crumble, reserving about 4 tablespoons of the bacon grease in the pan. Sauté the onion in the bacon grease over low heat for about 5 minutes, or until translucent. Remove onion from the pan and add to the crumbled bacon. Add the mustard to the pan and whisk together with the bacon grease and heat for 2-3 minutes. Turn off the heat and whisk in the vinegars, honey, salt and pepper. Remove the potatoes from the oven. Once cool enough to handle, peel and cut into 1/2 inch slices. In a large bowl, drizzle the dressing over the potato slices and gently toss with the bacon, sliced onion and chopped parsley. Adjust the seasoning and enjoy warm or at room temperature. The salad will taste better if it sits in the refrigerator for several hours before serving.

Sweet Potato Salad with Bacon Vinaigrette

The German-speaking countries are known for tasty potato salads seasoned with vinegary dressings and bacon or ham. This southern-inspired take on the Teutonic classic utilizes sweet potatoes for a flavorful salad that doubles as a versatile side dish as well.

Breads

Bourbon Brown Sugar Muffins
Page 79

2 cups self-rising flour
4 tablespoons brown sugar
1/2 teaspoon salt
1/4 teaspoon ground nutmeg
1/4 cup butter
1/4 cup lard
   (or shortening, if you must)
1 cup mashed sweet potatoes
6 tablespoons buttermilk

Sweet Potato Biscuits

Contrary to popular opinion, sweet potatoes and yams are not the same vegetable. They belong to completely different plant families – sweet potatoes are grown in the U.S., while yams are usually imported from the Caribbean – and the flavor and texture can vary greatly. Either will do in this southern-inspired biscuit recipe, but real sweet potatoes add that extra bit of Bluegrass flavor.

Combine flour, sugar, salt and nutmeg in a bowl. Cut in the butter and the lard until the mixture is somewhat crumbly. Add sweet potato and buttermilk, and gently stir until incorporated. Turn out onto a floured surface and knead gently to form a soft dough. Roll out to 1-inch thickness and cut out 2-inch rounds with a biscuit cutter. Place biscuits on a parchment-lined baking sheet and bake at 400 degrees for 12 minutes or until golden brown.

2 cups all-purpose flour
2 teaspoons baking powder
2 tablespoons sugar
1/2 teaspoon salt
1/4 cup butter
1 cup heavy whipping cream

Preheat oven to 425 degrees. Sift together the flour, baking powder, sugar and salt in a medium bowl. Cut in the butter until the mixture resembles cornmeal. Add cream and mix to form a soft dough. Turn out onto a surface dusted with additional flour and knead several times, adding just enough flour to keep dough from sticking. Gently roll out to 3/4-inch thickness and use a 2-inch biscuit cutter coated with flour to cut dough into biscuits. Place on a baking sheet lined with parchment paper, with at least 1-inch between each biscuit and bake for 10 minutes, or until golden brown.

Cream Biscuits

Biscuits have come to be known as the quintessential American quick bread, however, no other region in the U.S. has become so identified with the humble biscuit as the South. Smothered in milk or sausage gravy, slathered in butter or cushioning thin slices of salty country ham, Kentucky biscuits can come in many forms. Beaten, laced with buttermilk or sweet potato, biscuits in the Bluegrass can be found at breakfast, lunch or dinner. This elegant, yet simple, recipe gets its richness from fresh dairy cream.

4-6 cups all-purpose flour
2 envelopes dried yeast
2 tablespoons sugar
2 cups sour milk
1 tablespoon salt
1/4 cup honey
2 tablespoons melted butter

Sour Milk Rolls with Honey Glaze

Before the days when preprocessed foods and convenience took hold of American kitchens, thrift and economy were considered virtues in the domestic arts. Nothing was wasted, and even things like milk that had gone sour would be used in a multitude of tasty dishes. If you don't have any sour milk on hand, you can substitute buttermilk or 2 cups of whole milk plus 1/4 cup plain yogurt for this frugal recipe.

In a large bowl, combine together 4 cups of the flour, the yeast and sugar. Heat the milk to about 105 degrees and add to the flour mixture. Add the salt and mix well, adding additional flour as needed, to produce a moist dough. Turn out onto a well-floured surface and knead until firm and elastic. Place the dough in a large bowl that has been greased with a bit of olive oil or butter, cover with a damp towel and set in a warm place to rise for an hour. After the dough has risen, punch it down and turn it out onto the floured surface again. Divide the mass into 16 small pieces and roll each one into a smooth ball that is placed on baking sheets lined with parchment paper or in buttered muffin tins. Let rise for another half hour and bake in an oven at 400 degrees for 15 minutes or until golden brown. After the rolls have been removed from the oven, cool on a wire rack for 10 minutes and brush with the glaze that is made by combing the honey and butter.

4-6 cups all-purpose white flour
2 envelopes dried yeast
2 tablespoons sugar
2 cups lukewarm water
1/4 cup bourbon
1 tablespoon salt
1 cup shelled pumpkin seeds

In a large bowl, combine 4 cups of the flour, the yeast and sugar. Heat the water to about 105 degrees and add to the flour mixture. Add the bourbon, salt, and pumpkin seeds and mix well. Add additional flour as needed, to produce a moist dough. Turn out onto a well-floured surface and knead until firm and elastic. Place the dough in a large bowl that has been greased with a bit of olive oil or butter, cover with a damp towel and set in a warm place for an hour to rise. After the dough has risen, punch it down and turn it out onto the floured surface again. Divide the mass into 3 pieces and shape each one into a round loaf that is placed on a baking sheet lined with parchment paper. Dust the surface of each loaf with a bit of flour and make 3 diagonal slits across the top with a very sharp knife. Let rise for another 30 to 45 minutes and bake in a 400-degree oven for 25 minutes or until golden brown. After the loaves have been removed from the oven, cool on a wire rack.

Pumpkin Seed Loaves

Although pumpkins and squashes have played an important part in indigenous Bluegrass cuisine for thousands of years, many dishes employ the flavorful and nutritious flesh, rather than the seeds. Subtly sweet and nutty, the roasted kernels from the interior of the pumpkin happen to be one of the most nutritious and flavorful seeds around. Pumpkin seeds are flat and dark green, and in many cultures they figure prominently in the manufacture of tasty breads and rolls. This rustic recipe adds a flavorful twist to a traditional white bread and can be enjoyed any time of the day.

Sally Lunn

This rich, egg-based bread counts as another of those recipes that has fallen out of favor in many modern kitchen across the South, where at one time it was as prevalent as biscuits and barbecue. Originating in England – where a supposed young baker woman of either English or French extract hawked the brioche-like loaves on the streets of Bath – the recipe came to the New World by way of British colonists. Pioneers from Virginia brought the delicate bread to Kentucky, where it remained a Bluegrass favorite for many years.

4-6 cups all-purpose flour
2 envelopes dried yeast
1/2 cup sugar
1 1/2 cups lukewarm half-and-half
3 large eggs
1 tablespoon salt
2 tablespoons melted butter
1 tablespoon lemon zest

In a large bowl, combine 3 cups of the flour, yeast, sugar and half and half to make a thick batter. Let sit for 10 minutes or until bubbles start to form on the surface of the mixture. Beat in the eggs, salt, butter, lemon zest and enough flour to make a sticky dough. Turn out onto a well-floured surface and knead until firm and elastic. Place the dough in a large bowl that has been greased with a bit of olive oil or butter, cover with a damp towel and set in a warm place for an hour to rise. After the dough has risen, punch it down and turn it out onto the floured surface again. Divide the dough into 3 portions and shape each one into a round form. Place each in a lightly buttered 4-inch ovenproof bowl and let rise for another 30 minutes. Bake in a 400-degree oven for 20 minutes or until deep brown. After the loaves have been removed from the oven, cool on a wire rack.

For a decorative touch, cut a crescent moon shape out of waxed paper, lay on the surface of each loaf and dust with powdered sugar. Remove the paper and enjoy warm or at room temperature

Distiller's Baguettes

For generations, bakers in Europe have used the tasty spent grains from the distilling process to make hearty brown breads. Farmers and distillers in early Kentucky more often than not fed the nutritious leftovers to livestock; however, more and more Bluegrass bakers are discovering that distiller's flour, the ground grains from the dried sour mash used in bourbon production, makes the perfect base for wholesome breads with distinctive flavor. If you can't get your hands on distiller's flour, several varieties of mixes are available online or at gift shops.

4 cups distiller's flour
2 cups all-purpose flour
1/2 cup brown sugar
2 envelopes dried yeast
1 1/2 cups lukewarm water
1/4 cup vegetable oil
1 tablespoon salt

In a large bowl, stir together flours, sugar, yeast, water, oil and salt to make a sticky dough. Turn out onto a well-floured surface and knead until firm and elastic, adding additional flour if needed. Place the dough in a large bowl that has been greased with a bit of olive oil or butter, cover with a damp towel and set in a warm place for an hour to rise. After the dough has risen, punch it down and turn it out onto the floured surface again. Divide the dough into 2 equal portions and shape each one into a long, thick rope that is placed on a baking sheet lined with parchment paper. Make 4-6 parallel diagonal slits along the top of each loaf and let rise for another 30 minutes. Bake in a 400-degree oven for 15-20 minutes or brown and crusty. After the baguettes have been removed from the oven, cool on a wire rack and enjoy warm or at room temperature.

mallets and special-made machines, have been used to beat the dough over the years. Whichever tool you choose, it is sure to be a good stress-reliever.

4 cups all-purpose flour
1 teaspoon salt
1/4 cup lard
2 tablespoons unsalted butter
1 cup cold milk

Beaten Biscuits

Many people compare the dry texture of these Derby must-haves to flavorless hardtack, however, no cookbook featuring southern favorites would be complete without them. These traditional southern biscuits date back to days when baking powder and baking soda were unavailable. Pearlash, a popular leavener at the time, often gave breads a bitter taste, and cooks found that by folding and pounding unleavened biscuit dough enough times, they could use tiny air pockets formed in the dough to make it rise. Various implements including axe handles, rolling pins, wooden

Combine flour and salt in a bowl and add lard and butter. Using your fingertips or the tines of a fork, work lard and butter into flour mixture until it resembles coarse meal. Stir in the milk and mix well. Turn out onto a floured surface and knead until dough keeps its shape. Pat the dough out to 1-inch thickness and gently pound it with a rhythmic motion. When the surface has been well beaten, fold the dough in half and repeat the process. Continue for at least 20 minutes until the dough is well blistered. Roll out dough to a 1/2-inch thickness and cut into rounds with a small biscuit cutter, repeating until all dough has been used. Place on parchment-lined baking sheet, and prick the top of each biscuit several times with a fork. Bake in oven preheated to 400 degrees for 20 minutes or until golden brown around the edges. Beaten biscuits also make the perfect base for a wide assortment of Bluegrass canapes.

4 cups **Weisenberger Mills**
whole wheat flour
2 envelopes dried yeast
1 1/2 cups lukewarm water
1/2 cup sorghum
2 tablespoons flaxseed oil
(other vegetable oils will work)
2 cups all-purpose flour
1 tablespoon kosher salt

Combine whole wheat flour, yeast, water, sorghum and oil to make a sticky batter. Add all-purpose flour and turn out onto a well-floured surface and knead to make an elastic dough. Place the mass in a large bowl greased with a bit of olive oil, cover with a damp towel and set in a warm place to rise for an hour. After the dough has risen, punch it down and turn it out onto the floured surface again. Divide the dough into 12 portions and shape each one into a ball that is placed in oiled muffin tins or on baking sheets lined with parchment paper. Let rise for another 30 minutes and bake in an oven that has been preheated to 400 degrees for 15-20 minutes or until golden brown. After the loaves have been removed from the oven, cool on a wire rack and enjoy warm or at room temperature.

Sorghum Wheat Rolls

Sorghum and molasses have been popular sweeteners in the South for over a hundred years. Although the names are often interchanged, they are two distinct products. Molasses is a derivative of the sugar cane, whereas sorghum comes from a variety of grasses raised for grain. Sorghum – especially popular in Kentucky and Tennessee – compliments the natural sweetness of whole wheat in this recipe for brown rolls that can be used as a sandwich base or the perfect accompaniment for a hearty country meal.

White Corn Popovers

An American spin-off of Yorkshire pudding, an English cousin, popovers are made from an egg-based batter. When baked in an extremely hot oven, they rapidly expand and pop over the sides of the muffin cups to produce light and hollow rolls. They can be served by themselves at breakfast or lunch, or they can accompany hearty roasts and other meat-based dishes.

2 large eggs
1 1/2 cups milk
2 tablespoons melted butter
1/2 teaspoon salt
1 cup bread flour
1/4 cup fine white cornmeal

Set empty muffin tins in the oven and preheat to 450 degrees. In a large bowl, whisk together the eggs, milk, and butter. Add the salt, flour and cornmeal and mix until well blended. The batter should be very thin. Remove muffin cups from the oven and brush with melted butter and fill each with batter. If you have any unfilled muffin cups, fill them halfway with water. This will keep the pan from overheating and burning. Place filled muffin tins in the center rack of the oven and bake for 15 minutes or until they are golden brown and have popped over. Remove from the oven and serve warm. For a sweet treat, dust with confectioners' sugar and serve with fresh fruit.

2 cups distiller's flour or
    sour mash bourbon bread mix
1 cup all-purpose flour
3 teaspoons baking powder
1/2 teaspoon salt
1/4 cup lard or shortening
1/4 cup unsalted butter
2 tablespoons molasses
1/2 cup buttermilk

Combine the flours, baking powder and salt in a large bowl and cut in the shortening and butter until the mixture resembles a course meal. Combine the molasses and buttermilk and add to the flour mixture, stirring until incorporated. Turn out onto a floured surface and knead gently until the dough holds its shape. Roll out a large rectangle of about 1/2-inch thickness. Cut out small rounds or use the tines of a fork to score the surface of the dough and cut out rectangles that are 2 inches by 3 inches. Bake in a 425-degree oven for 12 minutes or until nicely browned.

Sour Mash Biscuits

After a trip to Maker's Mark Distillery in the 1990s when they were revamping the menu at the famous five-diamond Oakroom restaurant at the Seelbach Hilton in Louisville, then executive chef Jim Gerhardt and director of restaurants Adam Seger came up with the idea of using leftover sour mash to make a signature brown bread for the dining room. They teamed up with Early Times Bourbon Whiskey to create their popular Sour Mash Bourbon Bread Mix with its flavorful combination of ground corn, barley and wheat with slight bourbon nuances. The mix can be used to make wonderful biscuits as well.

Spoon Bread with Smoked Gouda and Green Onions

Although this classic Southern bread might be better classified as a side dish, spoon bread combines traditional bread-making ingredients with the ease and convenience of a casserole. It can be found as the signature dish on many menus in country inns and taverns across the Bluegrass, and this simple recipe uses Kenny's Farmhouse Smoked Gouda for an extra bit of flavor.

3 cups whole milk
1 1/2 cups white cornmeal
3 eggs, beaten
2 tablespoons melted butter
1 teaspoon salt
2 teaspoons baking powder
1/2 teaspoon ground white pepper
2 cups shredded smoked Gouda
1/2 cup chopped green onion

In a saucepan, bring the milk to a boil and stir in the cornmeal. Cook until the mixture has thickened and stir often to prevent sticking on the bottom. Remove from the heat and when the mixture has cooled, stir in the beaten eggs, butter, salt, baking powder and pepper until well blended. Add the cheese and onions, stir well and pour the mixture into a well-greased casserole. Bake in a 375-degree oven for 30-35 minutes and serve by the spoonful.

4 cups all-purpose flour
2 cups dark brown sugar
2 teaspoons baking powder
1 teaspoon cinnamon
1/2 teaspoon salt
2 cups milk
1/2 cup bourbon
1/4 cup vegetable oil
2 large eggs
1 tablespoon vanilla extract

Preheat the oven to 425 degrees.
In a large bowl, combine the dry
ingredients. Whisk together the
remaining ingredients in a separate
bowl and pour the liquid into the
bowl with the dry ingredients. Mix until
just moistened and spoon the mixture
into greased muffin cups and fill to
2/3 full. Bake for 15 minutes or until
the tops are firm and spring back when
dented with a finger.

Bourbon Brown Sugar Muffins

Many incorrectly believe that
brown sugar is actually a form of
raw or unprocessed sugar, but it
is usually nothing more than
refined white sugar with molasses
added to it. This rich flavor pairs
up nicely with good Kentucky
whiskey in this easy recipe that
can be enjoyed for breakfast,
lunch or dinner.

Main Courses

Bourbonnaised Filet Mignon
Pages 102 & 103

Free Range Chicken Breast with Caviar Sauce

This recipe is perfect for those who don't care for the flavor or texture of straight-up caviar. In a savory, cream-based sauce, it provides an elegant and tasty accompaniment to free-range Kentucky chicken breasts that have been broiled to crispy perfection. The stunning, full-flavored berries of Kinder Caviar – Caspian Sea style caviar made right here in the Bluegrass – add a stylish touch to this surefire hit.

6-8 free-range chicken breasts
1/4 cup bourbon
1/4 cup olive oil
1 teaspoon kosher salt
1/2 teaspoon black pepper
2 large shallots, diced
 (about 1/4 cup)
1 tablespoon butter
2 tablespoons Kentucky spoonfish
 caviar
1 cup sour cream
1/4 teaspoon grated nutmeg
Salt and pepper to taste
Sprigs of fresh thyme for garnish

Preheat the oven to 450 degrees. Arrange the chicken breasts in a large baking dish and drizzle with the bourbon and olive oil. Sprinkle with salt and pepper and bake for 20-25 minutes or until they turn golden brown. Turn off the oven and remove the baking dish. In a large skillet over medium heat, sauté the chopped shallot in the butter until translucent. Add the caviar, sour cream and nutmeg and stir until the sauce has heated all the way through. Add enough of the juices from the baking dish to produce the desired thickness and season with salt and pepper to taste. Before serving, place the chicken breasts under the broiler for several minutes until deep brown. Ladle a spoonful of the caviar sauce over each and serve garnished with sprigs of fresh thyme.

Chateaubriand with Henry Bain Sauce

For years, Chateaubriand of beef could be found on practically all
fine-dining menus across the U.S., where it was a favorite for couples
eating out. For whatever reason – perhaps the trend away from
French-inspired cuisine or the downsizing of portions – Chateaubriand
has more or less been relegated to the back pages of outdated menus
or else reserved as a highlight for special retro occasions. According to
Larousse Gastronomique, the personal chef of French author and
statesman François-René de Chateaubriand popularized this cut, which
is usually only offered as a serving for two, as there is only enough
meat in the center of the average fillet for two portions. Chateaubriand
is often grilled "barded," which refers to cooking with bacon wrapped
around it to keep it moist. It is usually served medium-rare and with
a sauce, and in Kentucky, it has to be served with Henry Bain Sauce.

1 cup bourbon
1/4 cup Worcestershire sauce
1/4 cup hot sauce
4-pound tenderloin of beef
Several sprigs of fresh rosemary
1 tablespoon kosher salt
1 tablespoon cracked black pepper

Combine the bourbon, Worcestershire and hot sauce in a shallow baking dish. Add the tenderloin and rosemary. Set the dish in the refrigerator to marinate for at least 2 hours, making sure to turn the beef several times to ensure an even marinade. Preheat the oven to 450 degrees, remove the tenderloin from the marinade and place in a roasting pan, surrounded by the sprigs of rosemary, on an upper rack in the oven. Season with the salt and pepper. Roast for about half an hour or until a meat thermometer stuck into the center reads 135 degrees. Baste with the leftover marinade every 10 minutes or so. Remove from the oven and allow to sit for 10 minutes before cutting into thick slices served with Henry Bain Sauce.

Henry Bain Sauce

A tangy, sweet-sour condiment invented by Henry Bain, the head waiter at the Pendennis Club in the 1880s, to compliment the wild game brought in by customers, this tomato-based Kentucky sauce has seen many spin-offs. Although no definitive recipe supposedly remains, this approximation does the original justice.

2 cups tomato ketchup
1 cup chili sauce
1 cup apricot preserves
1/2 cup finely chopped pecans
1 cup Worcestershire sauce
1/2 cup bourbon
1/4 cup brown mustard
1/4 cup hot sauce
1/2 cup apple cider vinegar
1/2 cup apple cider

Combine all the ingredients and purée in a blender.

Medallions of Pork with Green Peppercorn Bourbon Reduction

Good cooks in the Bluegrass have realized that bourbon enhances a wide variety of recipes and imparts a distinctive flavor to both sweet and savory dishes alike. Wild Turkey Rare Breed — with its notes of spicy clove, apricot and pepper — adds an elegant finish to this satisfying autumnal dish.

24-ounce pork tenderloin, cut into 1-inch slices
2 cups bourbon
1/4 cup green peppercorns
2 tablespoons olive oil
3 small shallots, finely diced
1 tablespoon brown mustard
1/2 cup heavy cream
1 teaspoon kosher salt
1/2 teaspoon ground white pepper

Marinate the pork medallions in a large bowl with the bourbon and peppercorns for 2 hours in the refrigerator; stir once every half hour to make sure all the pieces marinate evenly. Remove the medallions from the marinade and season with salt and pepper. Add the olive oil to a large skillet placed over medium heat and brown the medallions for 3-4 minutes on each side. After each one has browned, remove it to a large platter with the others and cover with foil to keep warm. In the same skillet, sauté the shallots until translucent and add the bourbon-peppercorn marinade. Turn up the heat and reduce the mixture by half. Whisk in the mustard and cream and cook until the mixture thickens. Season with salt and pepper to taste and return the medallions to the reduction until they have been warmed through. Serve surrounded by buttered limas and halved cherry tomatoes with rosemary roast potatoes or warm sweet potato salad.

Sweet Potato Dumplings with Turkey

Dumplings are another of those wonderful comfort-food items that have come to us by means of our colonial European ancestors, and their many variations across the country have come to represent the epitome of country cooking. In Kentucky, the savory varieties tend to be one of two sorts — *slick* or *runner* dumplings, which are actually more akin to thick noodles, and drop dumplings. This recipe uses the lighter *drop* variety flavored with the earthy goodness of sweet potatoes for a satisfying, down-home favorite.

1 boneless turkey breast,
   about 4 pounds
4 cups water
4 cups chicken broth
2 cups white wine
1 medium onion, roughly chopped
2 large bay leaves
2 teaspoons kosher salt
2 large carrots, diced
2 ribs of celery, diced
2 large potatoes, diced
2 cups mashed sweet potatoes
2 large eggs
1 cup milk
1 1/2 cups all-purpose flour
2 teaspoons baking powder
1 teaspoon kosher salt
1/2 teaspoon ground white pepper
1/4 teaspoon grated nutmeg
Chopped green onion or
   parsley for garnish

In a large stock pot, simmer the turkey, water, broth, wine, onion, bay leaves and salt for 90 minutes or until the turkey becomes tender and starts to fall apart. Add the carrots, celery, and potatoes during the last 30 minutes of cooking. Remove turkey from the broth and set aside until it is cool enough to shred. To make the dumplings, combine the sweet potatoes, eggs, milk, flour, baking powder and seasonings. Turn up the heat on the broth and bring to a low boil. Drop spoonfuls of the dumpling batter into the hot broth and cook for about 5 minutes or until the centers are light and fluffy. You may have to cook the dumplings in several batches. After the last batch is finished and the dumplings have been removed to a flat pan or baking dish, remove the bay leaves and return the turkey to the broth and vegetables. You may need to add more water or stock if the broth has evaporated or thickened too much. For each serving, ladle some of the turkey into a large bowl or soup plate and top with several of the dumplings. Garnish with chopped green onions or parsley and enjoy.

Molasses-Glazed Pork Chops with Caramelized Onions

The sticky syrup made from sugar cane reigned as the sweetener of choice in the U.S. until after World War I, when sugar prices dropped enough to knock it from its spot. It still retains a spot on the shelf in many pantries across the South, and in Kentucky it is especially prized for use in down-home recipes. Paired with the natural sweetness of caramelized onions and seared pork, the earthy goodness of molasses adds a flavorful dimension to this elegant dinner dish.

1 cup molasses
1 cup chicken stock
2 tablespoons bourbon
6-8 double-cut pork chops
   (12-16 ounces each,
   2 inches thick)
1 teaspoon kosher salt
1/2 teaspoon cracked black pepper
4 teaspoons olive oil
Sprigs of fresh rosemary
   for garnish

Prepare the glaze by combining the molasses, stock, bourbon and a pinch of salt in a heavy saucepan over medium heat. Bring to a boil and reduce the heat to medium-low and simmer about 30 minutes or until reduced to a thick syrup (about 1 cup). Remove from the heat. Season each chop on both sides with salt and pepper and sear for 3 minutes on each side in a hot skillet with the olive oil. Transfer to a baking sheet and broil for 5-6 minutes on each side or until cooked through (an instant-read thermometer inserted into the center should read 150 degrees). Place the chops on a serving dish and drizzle with the glaze. Garnish with fresh rosemary and serve with Savory Bourbon Whipped Sweet Potatoes and Caramelized Onions.

Caramelized Onions

4 tablespoons unsalted butter
4 tablespoons olive oil
2 pounds yellow onions,
   peeled and thinly sliced
1/2 teaspoon kosher salt
1/2 teaspoon ground white pepper

Melt the butter with the olive oil in a large skillet over medium-high heat. Add the onions and reduce the heat to low. Cook for 45 minutes to an hour, stirring occasionally, until golden brown and caramelized. Remove from the heat, season with salt and pepper and serve warm.

Beer-Braised Beef with Parsley Dumplings

Alltech Brewing Company in Lexington uses spent bourbon casks, fresh from decanting, to store its golden Kentucky Ale. Barrels that once held the finest bourbons impart the beer with subtle notes of vanilla and oak. These flavors accent the natural goodness of grain-fed Kentucky Angus beef in this slow-cooked dish that is served with fluffy dumplings enhanced with the light taste of fresh parsley.

5 pounds beef chuck roast
3 large carrots, diced
3 ribs of celery, diced
1 large onion, diced
2 large cloves of garlic, chopped
2 large bay leaves
2 teaspoons kosher salt
1/2 teaspoon black pepper
1/4 teaspoon ground sage
3 cups Kentucky Bourbon
　Barrel Ale
3 cups beef stock
2 1/2 cups all-purpose flour
1 cup cubed white bread
1 teaspoon baking powder
1/2 teaspoon salt
1/2 teaspoon ground white pepper
1/4 teaspoon grated nutmeg
1/4 cup chopped parsley
2 eggs, beaten
1/2 cup milk

Preheat the oven to 425 degrees and cut the beef into large chunks. Place the beef in a roasting pan and add the carrots, celery, onion, garlic, bay leaves, 2 teaspoons salt, black pepper, sage, ale and stock. Cover and cook for at least 90 minutes or until the beef has become very tender. In a large bowl, combine the flour, bread crumbs, baking powder, salt, pepper, nutmeg, parsley, eggs and milk. Uncover the roasting pan and drop tablespoon-size lumps of the batter into the braising liquid and cook for 10 minutes or until the dumplings have expanded a bit and appear light and fluffy. You can also use wet hands to roll the dumplings in small balls that are cooked in boiling chicken stock. Serve up large bowls of the beef and dumplings on their own, or else enjoy with a heaping mound of whipped potatoes on a large plate. Fresh radishes and chopped dill pickle make a nice accompaniment to this dish.

Spare Ribs and Onion Gravy

Spare ribs are a variety of pork ribs eaten in many different cultures around the world. The most inexpensive of pork ribs, they became especially popular throughout the American South where choicer cuts often were not available to African slaves. One popular Kentucky preparation involves slow cooking in a vinegar-based braise. The following recipe uses bourbon and onions for a flavorful take on a southern favorite.

**2 large yellow onions,
  peeled and thinly sliced
5 pounds pork spare ribs
2 cups bourbon
1 cup apple juice
1/4 cup apple cider vinegar
2 1/2 teaspoons kosher salt
1 teaspoon ground white pepper
1/4 cup all-purpose flour
1 cup chicken broth
Fresh sage for garnish**

Layer the onions in a roasting pan and arrange the spare ribs on top. Pour in the bourbon, apple juice and vinegar and sprinkle with salt and pepper. Cover (if the roaster doesn't have a lid, use aluminum foil) and cook in a 450-degree oven for 90 minutes. Turn off the heat and let sit in the oven for 20 minutes. Remove roasting pan from the oven and take the spare ribs out. Wrap in foil and keep warm on a baking sheet in the oven. Place the roasting pan on the stove over medium heat. When bubbles start to form around the edge, whisk together the flour and broth. Add to the onions and juices in the roasting pan and mix well. Turn off the heat when the mixture thickens. Correct the seasoning, remove the ribs from the oven and arrange on a large serving platter. Cover with the onion gravy and garnish with fresh sage leaves.

Henry McKenna Baked Chicken

Said to be "Kentucky's Finest Table Whiskey," Henry McKenna Bourbon traces its roots to Fairfield, where the distillery was founded in 1855. McKenna, an Irishman who migrated to America in the 1830s, supposedly enjoyed a weekly Sunday dinner of farm-raised chicken baked in whiskey according to an old family recipe, and many of his Bluegrass neighbors soon started adding whiskey to their poultry recipes as well. The peppery, fruity notes of this pleasant Bourbon from Heaven Hill Distilleries make the perfect accompaniment to oven-baked chicken in this simple recipe.

4 pounds chicken pieces
1 cup bourbon
2 tablespoons fresh lemon juice
Pinch of salt
1 cup flour seasoned with
** 1 teaspoon kosher salt**
1/2 cup melted butter
1/2 teaspoon ground white pepper
1/4 teaspoon ground marjoram
Lemon slices for garnish

Preheat the oven to 425 degrees. Toss together the chicken, bourbon, lemon juice, and a pinch of salt. Marinate in the refrigerator for at least two hours. Remove the chicken from the marinade and toss each piece in the seasoned flour to coat well. Pour the marinade in a large, shallow baking dish and arrange the chicken in one layer on top of it. Drizzle with the melted butter and sprinkle with the pepper and marjoram and bake in the oven for 45 minutes to an hour or until the pieces are brown and crispy. Garnish with slices of fresh lemon and enjoy with buttery mashed potatoes and black-eyed peas.

Catfish Cutlets with Bluegrass Tartar Sauce

No other fish has managed to capture such a true feeling of the South as the humble catfish. Cornmeal-coated and fried in hot oil, served with lemon wedges or hush puppies and cole slaw, the flavorful flesh of this unpretentious creature figures prominently on southern tables from Kentucky and the Carolinas to Texas and Florida. This recipe adds saltines to the cornmeal for a lighter breading and pairs the fried fish with a zesty tartar sauce for a tasty Bluegrass sensation.

Bluegrass Tartar Sauce

**8 skinless, boneless catfish fillets
    (10-12 ounces each)
1/2 cup buttermilk
1 cup cornmeal
1 cup crushed saltines
1/2 teaspoon kosher salt
1/2 teaspoon white pepper
1/2 teaspoon cayenne pepper
3 cups vegetable oil for frying**

**2 cups mayonnaise
2 tablespoons apple cider vinegar
2 tablespoons bourbon
1/4 cup chopped capers
1/4 cup chopped sweet pickle
    or pickle relish
2 hard-cooked eggs, chopped
2 tablespoons finely chopped
    parsley**

Cut each of the fillets in half and use a wooden mallet or a rolling pin to very gently flatten each piece into a uniform oval shape. Place the pieces in a shallow dish, pour the buttermilk over and let sit in the refrigerator for an hour. Heat the oil in a large skillet or frying pan over medium-high heat 10 or 15 minutes prior to frying. The oil should be hot enough that a small bit of cornmeal or raw fish sizzles when dropped into it. Remove the cutlets from the buttermilk and let the excess buttermilk drip off. Dredge each piece in a mixture made by mixing together the cornmeal, saltines, salt and peppers until well coated. Fry the cutlets in the hot oil until golden and crispy on each side. Drain on a paper towel and serve hot with Bluegrass Tartar Sauce.

Combine all of the ingredients and serve with hot catfish.

Country Ham Steaks with Red-Eye Gravy and Hoppin' John

Located in Bremen, Father's Country Hams are a Kentucky tradition that started back in 1840 when the Gattons began curing hams on the family farm. Today, each ham is carefully selected and sugar cured before it is hung from the rafters and aged for at least 18 months. Then, a slow-smoldering hickory fire that imparts each with its signature flavor smokes the hams for anywhere from 10 to 18 days. Thick steaks glazed with red-eye gravy and served with Hoppin' John make a perfect lunch on New Year's Day in the Bluegrass.

Hoppin' John

1/4 cup butter
6-8 slices country ham,
   about 1/4-inch thick
1 cup black coffee

2 cups frozen black-eyed peas
1 cup salted water
2 slices bacon, diced
1 cup white rice
1 1/2 cups chicken broth
1/2 teaspoon kosher salt

In a large, well-seasoned skillet, warm the butter over low heat. Make small slits in the ham steaks around the edges to keep them from curling while cooking. Place steaks in the pan and fry until the edges brown slightly; turn and cook the other side. Remove the steaks to a plate and keep warm. Add the brewed coffee to the skillet, raise the heat to high, and bring it to a boil. Cook until the liquid reduces by half and return the ham to the skillet. Warm through and serve immediately, glazed with the red-eye gravy.

Add the frozen peas to 1 cup of salted water in a saucepan and bring to a boil. Simmer for 30 minutes or until the peas are tender, adding water if necessary. In a separate pan, sauté the bacon over medium heat until almost crispy. Maintain the heat and add the uncooked rice, stirring well. Fry the rice in the bacon grease for 2-3 minutes, stirring constantly and add the broth and bring to a boil. Continue cooking rice, uncovered, over high heat for five minutes, stirring frequently to avoid sticking on the bottom. Drain the peas and add to the cooking rice. Cover and simmer together for 2-3 minutes, then remove from the heat and let sit for half an hour. Do not remove the cover. After the time is up, uncover and fluff the rice with a fork and add salt to taste.

Bourbonnaised Filet Mignon

In Kentucky, it's been said that we'll try splashing bourbon on almost anything, so it's not surprising to find a wealth of whiskey-inspired dishes across the state. However, little by little, bourbon is finding its way into more and more recipes across the nation. Similar to brandy in character, a well-aged bourbon can be used in many main course dishes, not to mention in an endless variety of desserts, sides and sauces. Used as a marinade for lean beef tenderloin, bourbon works as a natural tenderizer and flavor enhancer. For a great combination, try Laura's Lean Beef and Maker's Mark bourbon in this recipe.

Six to eight 4-ounce filet mignons
1 cup bourbon
1 tablespoon freshly squeezed
  lemon juice
2 tablespoons butter
1/2 teaspoon kosher salt
1 tablespoon light brown sugar
2 tablespoons brown mustard
3/4 cup heavy cream

Lay the filets in a single layer in a shallow dish and pour in the bourbon and lemon juice. Place the dish in the refrigerator and let marinate for at least four hours, turning each filet over at least once to ensure an even marinade. To cook the filets, melt the butter in a well-seasoned skillet over medium-high heat. Remove the beef from the marinade and pat dry with a paper towel. Season each side with salt and rub with a bit of the brown sugar. Once the butter has started to sizzle, sear each filet for about 4 minutes on each side. Remove the steaks to a plate and cover with aluminum foil to keep warm. To make the sauce, turn the heat under the skillet up to high and add the leftover bourbon marinade. Once it begins to boil, whisk in the mustard and cream and reduce the sauce by half. Correct the seasoning. Spoon over the filets and enjoy.

Pork Tenderloin with Spicebush Berries and Roast Potatoes

In colonial times, settlers often used the berries of the local spicebush in place of more expensive items like cloves and cinnamon. Also known as *Appalachian allspice*, dried spicebush berries have always flavored a variety of dishes in the kitchens of eastern Kentucky. Often used in sweet dishes and desserts, they can also be used to season any number of meats and wild game. Matched with the spicy and aggressive essence of Woodford Reserve Straight Kentucky Bourbon from the old Labrot & Graham Distillery in Versailles, dried spicebush berries add a distinctive flavor to this roast pork dish.

4-5 pound pork tenderloin
2 cups Woodford Reserve bourbon
2 tablespoons dried spicebush berries
1 teaspoon kosher salt
1/2 teaspoon cracked black pepper
6 large new red potatoes
3 tablespoons olive oil
1 teaspoon kosher salt

Marinate the pork in the bourbon and berries in a large resealable plastic bag in the refrigerator for at least two hours. Remove from the bag and place the tenderloin in a roasting pan along with the bourbon marinade. Sprinkle the roast with salt and pepper and place in an oven, preheated to 425 degrees, for 50 minutes. Clean the potatoes and cut into 1-inch chunks, toss in the olive oil with the salt and bake in a shallow dish for 40 minutes while the tenderloin cooks. Remove the tenderloin from the oven and let sit for 10 minutes before slicing and serving with the crispy roast potatoes.

Chicken in Red Wine with Homemade Egg Noodles

One of the first attempts at commercial wine growing in the U.S. occurred in Kentucky in 1799, with plantings by the Kentucky Vineyard Society in Jessamine County. By the mid-1800s the Bluegrass state counted as the third largest wine-producing state in America. However, Prohibition would lead to the unfortunate demise of the booming industry. But, since the decline of the tobacco industry, Kentucky agriculture has been looking back to its early history for a new cash crop. Springhill Winery in Bloomfield was one of the first Kentucky wineries to capitalize on the long-lost tradition of Bluegrass winemaking, and its cabernet franc makes a perfect wine for cooking as well as enjoying on its own. It displays rich, fruity notes with black cherry overtones and light tannins that marry nicely with this coq-au-vin-inspired dish.

3 pounds chicken pieces
1 teaspoon kosher salt
1/2 teaspoon ground black pepper
1/2 cup all-purpose flour
3 tablespoons extra-virgin olive oil
1 bottle Springhill Vineyard
Cabernet Franc or dry red wine
2 bay leaves
2 large shallots, minced

Season the chicken parts with salt and pepper and toss in the flour to coat well. On the stove over medium heat, heat the olive oil in a large Dutch oven or covered cooking pan. Brown the chicken pieces on all sides, doing so in batches if necessary, and return all the pieces to the pan. Add the wine, bay leaves, shallots, and any flour left over from the coating process. Cover and place in a 425-degree oven for 90 minutes. Remove the lid during the last 15 minutes of cooking. Remove from the oven, correct the seasoning and serve with buttered Homemade Egg Noodles.

Homemade Egg Noodles

3 cups all-purpose flour
1 teaspoon kosher salt
6 egg yolks, beaten
1 teaspoon olive oil
1 tablespoon butter

Stir together the flour and salt in a large stainless steel bowl. Make a well in the center of the flour mixture and add the egg yolks and olive oil, using a fork to gradually work in the flour around the edges until well incorporated. If the dough appears too dry or too wet, you may add additional flour or water as needed. Turn out onto a lightly floured surface and knead the dough until elastic and pliable. Roll out to 1/8-inch thickness and cut the sheet into 2-inch by 2-inch squares, rerolling the scraps until all the dough has been used up. Stack the squares of pasta one atop the other and use a sharp knife to cut into eight 1/8-inch strips. Use your fingers to separate the noodles and drop into a large pot of salted boiling water. Cook for about a minute, or until the noodles float to the surface. Use a slotted spoon or hand-held sieve to drain the noodles and remove them to a large bowl. Toss with 1 tablespoon of butter or olive oil and add salt and pepper to taste. If desired, garnish with fresh peas, pearl onions and diced red pepper.

Pulled Pork with Pawpaw Barbecue Sauce

Said to be the origin of modern barbecue, Carolina-style pulled pork has evolved as one of the most predominant barbecue items in the Southeast. Cooking methods and recipes vary from region to region, however, one thing remains constant: the meat must be slow cooked long enough so that the pork is tender enough to pull apart with your fingers. Add a piquant, vinegary sauce made with pawpaw, also known as the Kentucky banana, and this down-home favorite is sure to please. A healthy dose of ground spicebush, an Appalachian favorite, rounds out the sauce.

5 pounds pork shoulder, bone in
1 cup bourbon
2 large bay leaves
1 1/2 teaspoons kosher salt
1 teaspoon black pepper
3 cups apple cider vinegar
1 cup puréed pawpaws
1 cup ketchup
1/2 cup honey
2 tablespoons prepared mustard
2 tablespoons
  Worcestershire sauce
1 tablespoon dried spicebush
1 teaspoon kosher salt
1/2 teaspoon cayenne pepper

Place the pork in a roasting pan with the bourbon and bay leaves. Sprinkle with salt and pepper, cover and place in an oven preheated to 500 degrees. After 30 minutes, reduce the heat to 250 degrees and slow roast for another 6 hours. Remove the pan from the oven and allow meat to cool. Once it's cool enough to handle, use a fork or fingers to shred the meat, discarding the bone and excess fat. If necessary, reduce the liquid in the roasting pan down to about 1/2 cup and return the shredded pork to the roasting pan and toss in the pan drippings to coat well; cover and set aside. To make the barbecue sauce, combine the vinegar, pawpaws, ketchup, honey, mustard, Worcestershire sauce, spicebush, salt and pepper in a large saucepan over medium-low heat and simmer for about an hour or until the sauce has reduced by 1/3. Strain out the spicebush and let cool. Warm the pulled pork and serve heaped on a plate with potato salad and cole slaw or sandwiched between sour mash rolls.

Pot Roast and Coffee Gravy

Surprisingly enough, fresh brewed coffee can enhance the flavors of a wide variety of savory dishes, including those with meats and vegetables. Many in the Bluegrass enjoy country ham steaks with red-eye gravy, but how many realize the thin, flavorful sauce is actually made from coffee? Pot roast, another old-time favorite, uses coffee to boost the rich flavors of slow-simmered beef that is best served with creamy mashed potatoes or buttered noodles.

4 to 5 pound beef chuck roast
1/2 cup flour
1 teaspoon kosher salt
1/2 teaspoon freshly ground black pepper
1/4 cup olive oil
1 red onion, coarsely chopped
2 large shallots, chopped
1/2 cup diced carrot
1/2 cup diced celery
4 bay leaves
1 teaspoon dried thyme
2 cups chicken or beef stock
2 cups freshly brewed coffee
1/2 cup bourbon
Salt and freshly ground pepper, to taste

Coat the roast with the flour seasoned with salt and pepper. Heat the oil in a large, heavy ovenproof pan over medium heat and add the roast and brown on all sides. Remove the meat from the pan and set aside. Add onion, shallots, carrots and celery to the skillet and sauté over medium heat until the onion is translucent. Return the roast to the skillet; add bay leaves, thyme, stock, coffee and bourbon. Bring to a simmer and make sure the roast has been turned over in the pan to mix all the ingredients. Cover with a lid or foil and bake in a 325-degree oven. After 3 hours or so, the beef should be fork tender. Uncover and remove the roast from the pan; cover with foil to keep warm. Set the pan over medium heat (there should be at least 2 cups of liquid – if not, add juice or stock as needed.) Whisk 2-3 tablespoons of the flour leftover from coating the roast in the pan and cook about 5 minutes until smooth and thickened. Season with salt and pepper and return the roast to the pan to warm in the gravy. If desired, garnish with chopped parsley.

Guinea Hen with Ginger

Guinea hens belong to a family of birds similar to pheasants and turkeys that is native to Africa. How they ended up in Kentucky is a mystery to many people, however, Angela Benz' farm in Washington County (Poultry in Motion) provides a constant supply of these tasty, chicken-like fowl to residents of the Bluegrass on a year-round basis. Paired with fresh ginger, a true Bluegrass native, roast guinea hen offers a nice alternative to the standard Kentucky fried chicken.

2 fresh guinea hens
1/4 cup fresh grated ginger
4 large bay leaves
2 large navel oranges
1 cup apple cider
1 teaspoon kosher salt
Fresh sliced ginger

Preheat the oven to 425 degrees. Clean the guinea hens and stuff each one with half the grated ginger, 2 bay leaves and an orange that has been quartered. Transfer to a covered roasting pan, pour in the apple cider and sprinkle the hens with the salt. Roast, covered, for an hour to 75 minutes until golden brown. When pierced with a sharp knife or fork, the hens should release juices that run clear. If desired, garnish each bird with slices of fresh Kentucky ginger.

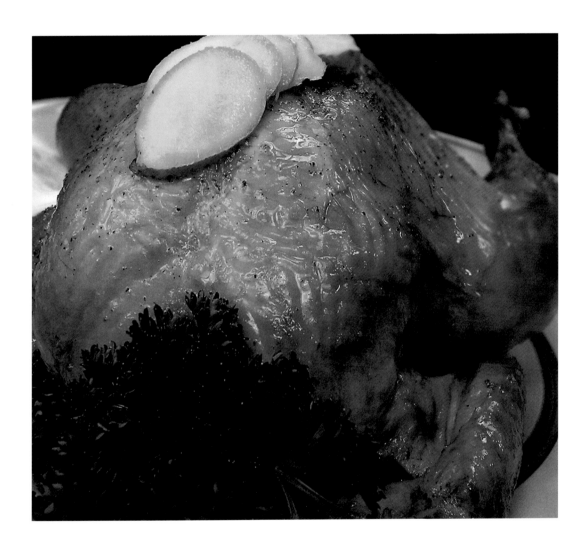

Barded Meat Loaf

For those not daunted by the recent anti-fat jihad, barded meat loaf can offer a tasty alternative to a standard meat loaf recipe. *Barding* refers to the practice of wrapping meat in fat such as bacon to avoid drying out and burning during the cooking process; however, it also adds an enormous amount of flavor. This recipe lightens up the traditional all-beef loaf with the addition of ground pork and turkey studded with chopped dill pickle.

3 pounds ground beef
1 pound ground pork
1 pound ground turkey
4 eggs, slightly beaten
1 cup rolled oats
1 cup chopped dill pickle
1 medium onion, finely chopped
1/2 cup chopped green onion
4 tablespoons hot sauce
4 tablespoons
   Worcestershire sauce
2 tablespoons brown mustard
2 tablespoons chopped capers
1 tablespoon kosher salt
1 tablespoon ground black pepper
10-12 strips of smoked bacon
Bay leaves and juniper berries
   for decoration

Preheat the oven to 350 degrees. Combine all the ingredients except the bacon, bay leaves and juniper berries and mix well. Divide the mixture into two equal portions and form into oblong loaves on greased baking sheets. Lay strips of bacon across each to form a crisscross pattern and decorate with bay leaves and juniper berries. Bake in the oven for 20 minutes, then remove and allow to cool for 20 minutes; bake for another 30 minutes and then remove and let cool for 20 minutes. This will allow the meat loaves to cook evenly and will avoid cracks and breaks in the surface. Reheat in the oven for 15-20 minutes prior to serving and slice and serve. This recipe will make enough to have enough leftovers for tasty meat loaf sandwiches the next day.

Sides

White Asparagus Vinaigrette
with Country Ham Crumbles
Page 123

Savory Bourbon Whipped Sweet Potatoes

Side dishes with sweet potatoes in the South all too often emerge heavily laden with brown sugar, molasses or other gooey sweeteners that mask the natural sugars of this healthful tuber. This savory recipe plays up a traditional mashed potato preparation with a healthy dose of bourbon that accents the inherent goodness of the sweet potato rather than cover it up. The mellow combination of sweet aromas with the rich, spicy flavors of Four Roses Small Batch Bourbon make it a logical choice for this recipe.

6 large sweet potatoes, peeled and cut in cubes
1/2 cup unsalted butter
1/2 cup bourbon
1/4 cup cream
1 tablespoon kosher salt
1 teaspoon ground white pepper
1/4 teaspoon grated nutmeg

Cook the potatoes in a large pot of salted water over medium heat for 30 minutes or until they are tender enough to pierce with a fork. Drain off the water and return the potatoes to the pot. Add the butter, bourbon, cream, salt and spices and whip together with a hand-held mixer until light and fluffy, adding more cream (or bourbon) as necessary. Correct the seasoning and enjoy.

Trappist Scalloped Potatoes

8 large new red potatoes,
  peeled and thinly sliced
1 1/2 teaspoons kosher salt
1/2 teaspoon ground white pepper
1/4 cup all-purpose flour
1/2 cup butter
2 cups shredded Trappist cheese
1 cup heavy cream

Preheat the oven to 400 degrees. Grease a baking dish or deep casserole and place a layer of potato slices on the bottom of the dish. Sprinkle with a dash of salt and pepper, a spoonful of flour and 2-3 pats of butter. Top with a handful of cheese and repeat the process until all the potatoes, cheese, butter, flour, salt and pepper have been used, but making sure to finish with a layer of potatoes. Pour the cream over the potatoes and cover the dish with aluminum foil. Bake for 45 minutes. Remove the foil, stir the potatoes and bake for another 20-30 minutes or until the top is bubbly and brown.

In 1848, 44 monks from a monastery in western France found a new home in the hills of central Kentucky where they founded the Abbey of Gethsemani. Their farming operations gradually grew to include the production and sale of bourbon fruit cakes, fudge and cheese. Using milk from their own herd of prize-winning Holsteins, the monks at Gethsemani Farms produce Bluegrass cheese in the tradition of their Trappist brothers at the Abbey of Port du Salut, the French monastery that lent its name to a world-renowned semi-soft cheese. Today the Trappist monks offer three distinct varieties of gourmet cheese: mild, aged, and smoky. The aged works best in this tangy variation of traditional scalloped potatoes.

Corn Pudding with Lovage and Country Ham

Lovage is a perennial herb native to the mountainous areas of southern Europe and Asia Minor that has been valued for its medicinal qualities and intense flavor for thousands of years. Once commonplace in many American herb gardens, it fell out of favor with gardeners for a time, but has gradually been making a comeback – especially in the South. The plant can grow up to six feet tall and has leafy stalks that resemble celery. The flavor – surprisingly enough strongly reminiscent of celery – adds a fresh twist to this old favorite.

4 cups frozen corn kernels,
   thawed and drained
1 cup chopped country ham
2 tablespoons chopped lovage
   (substitute 1/4 cup chopped
   celery leaves)
1/2 teaspoon kosher salt
1/2 teaspoon white pepper
6 large eggs
1 cup heavy cream

In a large bowl, combine the corn, ham, lovage, salt and pepper. In a separate bowl, whisk together the eggs and cream. Add to the corn and mix well. Pour into a greased casserole dish and cover with aluminum foil. Bake in a 375-degree oven for 30 minutes. Uncover and bake for another 15 minutes or until the top is golden brown.

8 large new red potatoes
1/2 cup butter
1/2 cup sliced shallots
1/4 cup bourbon
1 teaspoon kosher salt
1/2 teaspoon white pepper
1 cup heavy cream, scalded
Fresh chives for garnish

Smashed New Red Potatoes with Shallots and Whiskey Butter

Wash the potatoes and cut in eighths, leaving on the skins. Cook in salted boiling water for 30 minutes or until the potatoes are tender. While the potatoes are cooking, add the butter and shallots to a skillet or sauté pan and heat over medium heat, stirring often, until the butter has turned brown and the shallots are slightly caramelized. Carefully add the bourbon, turn up the heat until the bourbon starts to boil, then turn off the heat. Drain the water from the potatoes and use a potato masher to break the cooked potatoes into pieces. Add half of the butter-and-shallot mixture, salt, pepper and cream and continue mashing the potatoes. Scoop the potatoes into a large serving dish and top with remaining shallot-butter mixture. Garnish with chopped chives and cracked black pepper, and enjoy.

True to form, Kentuckians will use bourbon in all aspects of cooking. Although many might not suspect that whiskey and potatoes make a good match, bourbon adds a flavorful zing to sturdy new red potatoes when mashed together with creamery fresh butter and caramelized shallots.

1 cup heavy cream
1/4 cup all-purpose flour
1 1/2 teaspoons sea salt
1/2 teaspoon ground white pepper
1/4 teaspoon ground nutmeg
6 large sweet potatoes,
   peeled and thinly sliced
1 large red onion, peeled and
   thinly sliced
2 cups grated Cheddar cheese
   (such as Kenny's Farmhouse
   White Cheddar)

Sweet Potato Gratin with Red Onions and White Cheddar

Anyone who eats in the South knows that sweet potatoes have a wide variety of uses. Whether laced with sweet cream and maple syrup in pies, sweetened in casseroles with marshmallows, or adding flavor to biscuits and dumplings, sweet potatoes have a tendency to creep into most types of culinary occasions in states from Kentucky to Florida. This savory, upscale dish features tangy white Cheddar cheese and can be used as a flavorful side as well as a vegetarian-friendly main course.

Whisk together the cream, flour, salt, pepper and nutmeg to form a slurry. Layer slices of sweet potato, red onion, grated cheese and cream mixture in a heavily buttered casserole or baking dish. Cover and bake in at 400 degrees for 40 minutes or until hot and bubbly. Remove the foil and place the dish under a broiler for 5 or 10 minutes, until the top is browned and crusty. Remove from the oven and let sit for 10 minutes or so before serving.

White Asparagus Vinaigrette with Country Ham Crumbles

The appearance of asparagus used to be considered a harbinger of spring, but nowadays it is available practically any time of year. It is actually the sweet, tender, early shoot of a plant in the lily family and has a flavor like no other. Although the most common variety is the long green kind, Bluegrass asparagus comes in three colors: green, white, and purple. White asparagus is simply green asparagus that has been covered with soil during the growing process to blanch out the color. The flavor is about the same, but the texture is often more tender and perfect for elegant dishes like this Bluegrass original.

1 1/2 pounds fresh asparagus, cleaned and trimmed
2/3 cup extra-virgin olive oil
1/3 cup red wine vinegar
1 tablespoon brown mustard
1/2 teaspoon kosher salt
1/2 teaspoon cracked black pepper
1/4 teaspoon dried oregano
1 tablespoon minced shallot
1 cup roughly diced country ham

Brush the asparagus spears with a bit of olive oil, sprinkle with a pinch of salt and place on a hot grill for 2 minutes on each side. Remove and place on a serving dish. To make the vinaigrette, whisk together the vinegar, mustard, salt, pepper, oregano and shallot until incorporated. Slowly drizzle in all but a tablespoon of the olive oil in a thin stream, continually whisking until the mixture has emulsified. To prepare the crumbles, heat the remaining tablespoon of olive oil in a heavy skillet over medium heat and fry the country ham until brown and crispy. Remove the pieces and drain on a paper towel. To assemble the dish, drizzle the vinaigrette over the grilled asparagus and sprinkle with the country ham crumbles. Enjoy warm or cold.

1/2 cup chopped black walnuts
1/4 cup canola oil
3 tablespoons balsamic vinegar
2 tablespoons fresh lemon juice
1/2 teaspoon kosher salt
1/4 teaspoon ground black pepper
4 cups black-eyed peas, cooked
   and drained
1 teaspoon freshly chopped parsley
1 teaspoon freshly chopped chives

Black-Eyed Peas with Walnut Dressing

The black walnut is native to eastern North America, and extraction of the fruit of the black walnut is very difficult. In Kentucky, they are prized for their use in cookies and cakes, however, with the exception of the occasional salad, they are hardly ever used in savory recipes. This simple dish can double as a salad or side and can be served either warm or cold.

Preheat a heavy cast iron skillet over medium heat and toast the walnuts in a tablespoon of the canola oil until they are slightly brown and crispy. In a blender, purée 2 tablespoons of the walnuts with the vinegar, lemon juice, salt and pepper. Continue blending and slowly drizzle in the oil to form a smooth emulsion. In a large bowl, toss the cooked black-eyed peas with the dressing, the remaining walnuts and the parsley and chives. Adjust the seasoning and serve. This will taste better if allowed to sit for an hour or two before serving.

Spinach and Sweet Potato Soufflé

The word soufflé comes from the French verb "to blow up," and of all those imports from classical French culinary tradition, soufflés, have enjoyed an especially daunting reputation in this country. Although the basic concept behind the fluffy, feather-light dish is rather simple – combine beaten egg whites with a flavored base and bake – many American cooks find the soufflé experience a trying one. This savory recipe with spinach and sweet potato is a sturdier version of the classic French soufflé and can double as an elegant side dish or a light main course.

3 cups room temperature
  mashed sweet potatoes
6 large eggs, separated
1/2 cup unsalted butter, softened
1/2 cup heavy cream
1 teaspoon kosher salt
1/4 teaspoon ground white pepper
1/4 teaspoon grated nutmeg
1 cup chopped, frozen spinach

Preheat the oven to 400 degrees. Whip potatoes with an electric mixer. Add the egg yolks, butter, cream, salt, pepper and nutmeg and continue mixing well. Thaw the spinach and squeeze out any excess moisture. Add the chopped spinach to the whipped potatoes and mix. Whisk the egg whites until stiff peaks form and gently fold the potato-spinach mixture into them until incorporated. Pour into a large ramekin or baking dish that has been greased and floured. Bake for 20 minutes or until the soufflé has browned and risen dramatically. Serve warm.

Skillet Green Beans with Parsnips, Sweet Red Pepper and Bacon

Although the tough thread has been bred out of most varieties on the market today, the string bean name has stuck because they at one time had a tough fiber or "string" that ran from one tip to the other. There are several varieties of this popular garden vegetable; however, they're generally divided into two categories – bush beans, with a rounded pod, and pole beans, which are usually large and relatively flat. Kentucky Wonder has always been considered one of the best pole varieties, and it has a bright green bean that can reach six inches in length. When young, Kentucky Wonders have a sweet taste and an excellent, crisp texture that make them the perfect green bean for this hearty side dish.

2 pounds fresh green beans
12 strips hickory smoked bacon, chopped
1 cup fresh parsnip, peeled and cut in 1/4-inch cubes
2 large red peppers, seeded and cut in 1/4-inch strips
1/2 teaspoon kosher salt
1/2 teaspoon cracked black pepper
2 tablespoons apple cider vinegar

Wash the green beans and snap the ends off. Heat a cast-iron skillet over medium heat and add the bacon. Cook until the bacon is almost crispy and add the parsnips, peppers and green beans to the skillet. Sauté for 5-10 minutes, stirring frequently, and add the salt and pepper. Reduce the heat and add the vinegar. Cover and cook the beans for 15-20 minutes or until the beans and parsnips are tender. Correct the seasoning and serve.

2 pounds fresh carrots
2 tablespoons olive oil
1 teaspoon kosher salt
1/2 teaspoon cracked black pepper
1/4 cup butter
2 tablespoons bourbon
2 tablespoons honey
Chopped tarragon or parsley
    for garnish

Oven-Roasted Carrots with Honey and Bourbon

Preheat the oven to 425 degrees. Scrub the carrots and wash under cold running water. It is not necessary to peel them, however you may want to trim the stem end. Lay the carrots on a baking sheet and drizzle with the olive oil; season lightly with half the salt and pepper. Bake for about 25 minutes or until the carrots start to brown and blister. Remove from the oven and allow to cool for a minute or so. Use a sharp knife to cut the carrots on the diagonal in thick slices and transfer to a large bowl. Add the butter, bourbon, honey and remaining salt and pepper and toss well until the carrots are coated with a clear glaze. Serve immediately garnished with chopped tarragon or parsley and enjoy.

Carrots have a natural sweetness that pairs nicely with the sweet flavors of Kentucky bourbon, and oven roasting adds caramelization to these healthful, versatile vegetables. Finished off with a bit of butter and honey, this dish makes a wonderful accompaniment to almost any meal.

Coalminer's Beans

Pinto beans are an Appalachian specialty and in eastern Kentucky, they are often cooked simply and served with corn bread as a filling lunch or dinner at home or at work. Often referred to as soup beans, they were the traditional staple of early coalminers, and today they persist as one of the most common mountain dishes in the Bluegrass.

1 pound dried pinto beans
8 cups water or chicken broth
1 ham hock or
  1 cup chopped salt pork
2 large white onions, chopped
1/2 teaspoon ground pepper

Soak the pintos in warm water for 6-8 hours; drain and transfer to a large soup pot. Add the 8 cups water or broth and bring to a low rolling bowl over medium-high heat. Add the pork, onions and pepper. Reduce the heat and simmer for 2 hours, covered, or until the beans are tender. Correct the seasoning with additional salt and pepper if necessary, and enjoy. Depending on the consistency, these beans can be served as a hearty soup or side dish.

6 **large sweet potatoes, peeled
  and cut into 1/2-inch chunks**
4 **tablespoons butter**
2 **tablespoons olive oil**
1 **cup diced country ham**
1 **red onion, chopped**
2 **cloves garlic, minced**
1 **tablespoon fresh thyme**
1 **teaspoon kosher salt, if needed**
1 **teaspoon black pepper**
1/2 **teaspoon grated nutmeg**

Bring a pot of water to a boil and add the sweet potatoes, parboiling for 10 minutes. Remove from heat and drain. Melt the butter with olive oil in a sauté pan over medium-high heat and fry the ham pieces until slightly crispy. Add the onion and sauté until translucent, and then add the sweet potatoes. Fry over medium heat for 15-20 minutes, stirring often and adding the garlic during the last five minutes of cooking. Add the spices, mix well and serve.

Sweet Potato Hash

Sweet potato hash is down-home country fare for many in the South. Alongside scrambled eggs and buttermilk biscuits, it makes a satisfying and filling breakfast. Topped with a poached egg and with a simple green salad, it can be enjoyed as a light lunch. Served with peppered rib-eye steaks or roast pork tenderloin, sweet potato hash makes the perfect side dish.

Sweets

Chocolate Bourbon Gingerbread
Pages 144 & 145

Flourless Bourbon Chocolate Cake

Bourbon possesses a natural sweetness that makes it a perfect match with dessert. In cooking sweet dishes, the rich caramel and vanilla notes of many brands of bourbon whiskey enhance the flavor of chocolate. This decadent chocolate cake shines when paired with Old Forester, "the bourbon of Louisville." The "original bottled bourbon," Old Forester was founded on Louisville's Whiskey Row on Main Street in the 1870s, and it is still distilled and bottled there today.

1 cup unsalted butter, softened
1 cup granulated sugar
8 eggs, separated
10 ounces bittersweet chocolate
1/2 teaspoon salt
1 tablespoon vanilla extract
1/4 cup bourbon

Preheat the oven to 325 degrees. Cream the softened butter with 1/2 cup of the sugar until light and fluffy. Continue beating and add the egg yolks one at a time, making sure to scrape the sides of the bowl with a rubber spatula to ensure a smooth, even mixture. Melt the chocolate in the top of a double boiler until free of lumps and set aside. Use a clean bowl and beaters to whip the egg whites until stiff peaks form. Add the remaining sugar, salt and the vanilla extract to the egg whites and mix well. Once the chocolate has cooled slightly, return to the butter mixture and resume beating, slowly adding the melted chocolate. Once the chocolate is incorporated, add the bourbon and mix well. Fold the chocolate mixture into the egg whites and pour the batter into a buttered and floured spring-form pan. Bake in the oven for about 50 minutes, or until the cake has risen and the surface has started to crack. Turn off the heat and allow the cake to sit in the cooling oven for another 30 minutes. Remove from the oven, cover with aluminum foil and let cool completely. Remove from the form, slice and serve. If desired, garnish the top of the cake with fresh raspberries dusted with powdered sugar and serve on a large plate drizzled with chocolate sauce and strawberry coulis.

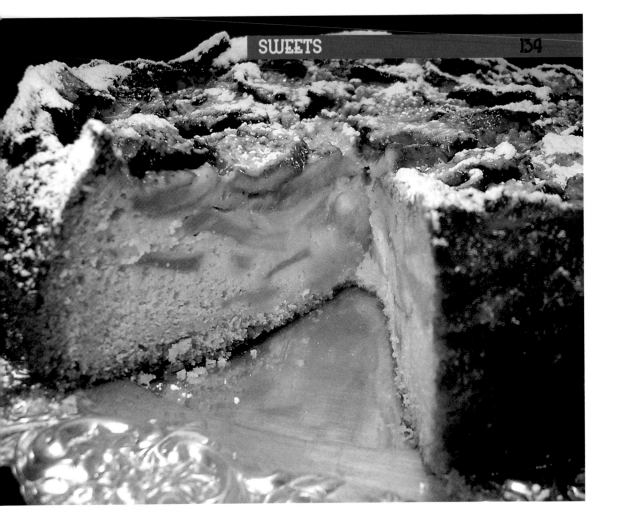

Four Roses Apple Kuchen

German immigrants to 19th-century Kentucky brought many of their culinary traditions to the Bluegrass, and one of them can be found in many bakeries across the state to this day. Known as *Apfelkuchen*, or apple cake, in German, this buttery pastry combines the best qualities of a cake and pie for a mouth-watering sweet that can be served any time of day. Said to be one of the mellowest spirits distilled in the U.S., Four Roses Bourbon of Lawrenceburg adds a distinctive flavor to this rich cake. Serve it warm with homemade vanilla ice cream or serve it at room temperature with bourbon whipped cream.

1 cup unsalted butter, softened
1 cup granulated sugar
4 large eggs
2 cups sifted all-purpose flour
1 teaspoon salt
1 teaspoon baking powder
1/2 teaspoon baking soda
1 tablespoon vanilla
1/2 cup Four Roses Bourbon
1/2 cup buttermilk
8 large, tart apples, peeled,
   cored and thinly sliced
2 tablespoons lemon juice
1/2 cup brown sugar
1/4 cup all-purpose flour
1/2 teaspoon ground cinnamon
1/4 teaspoon salt

Preheat oven to 375 degrees. Cream the butter and sugar together until light and fluffy using an electric mixer. Add the eggs, one at a time, and continue mixing. Sift together the flour, salt, baking powder and baking soda. Add to the butter mixture along with the vanilla extract, bourbon and buttermilk. Mix only until well incorporated and free of large lumps. The batter should be very thick and dough-like. Spoon it into a spring-form pan that has been greased and floured and spread it out. Toss the apple slices with the lemon juice, brown sugar, flour, cinnamon and salt in a separate bowl until well coated. Spoon over batter mixture in the cake pan. Use the back of the spoon to press the apple mixture down a bit. Bake, covered with aluminum foil, for 30 minutes. Remove the foil and bake for another 15-20 minutes until golden brown or a toothpick inserted in the center comes out clean. Remove from the oven, cover with the foil again, and allow to cool. Dust with powdered sugar, if desired, and serve with hand-whipped cream laced with bourbon.

Lemon Lavender Crème Brûlée with Bourbon Snaps

The decadent custard-like sweet known in French as crème brûlée has dominated the dessert lists of fine-dining restaurants across the U.S. for the last couple of decades. Although the Spanish and the French both take credit for inventing it, many credit the English as the inspiration for the slightly sweet, silky concoction with the caramelized sugar crust. Already in the 1600s, British college students supposedly gave it the original English name that would yield the popular French translation: burnt cream or burn custard. In parts of the Bluegrass, the old name still remains, however, most refer to it as crème brûlée today. Here, it is paired with thin spice cookies laced with the sparkle of bourbon.

2 cups heavy cream
2 tablespoons dried lavender
3 tablespoons grated lemon zest
8 egg yolks
1/4 cup granulated sugar
2 tablespoons honey
1/4 teaspoon kosher salt
1/2 teaspoon vanilla extract

Heat the cream with the lavender and lemon zest in a saucepan over low heat for 10-15 minutes, careful not to bring to a boil. Remove from the heat and allow to cool. Whisk the egg yolks, sugar and honey together in a large stainless-steel bowl until pale yellow and frothy. Strain the cooled cream and add to the egg mixture along with the salt and vanilla extract and whisk together. Strain the mixture once again to remove any lumps or impurities and divide the mixture between 8 ramekins or individual pudding cups. Place the ramekins in a bain-marie, or hot water bath, and carefully place in an oven preheated to 290 degrees for about an hour. Turn off the heat and let sit for another hour or so in the oven or until the individual crème brûlées have set and appear firm. Once cooled, remove from the oven, dust each one with a bit of granulated sugar and use a broiler or small torch to caramelize the sugar coating on top of each. Serve with Bourbon Snaps and enjoy.

Bourbon Snaps

1/2 cup butter, melted and cooled
1/2 cup brown sugar
1/4 cup molasses
1/4 cup bourbon
1 1/2 cup all-purpose flour
1/2 teaspoon kosher salt
1 teaspoon ground ginger
1/4 teaspoon ground cinnamon
1/4 teaspoon ground nutmeg
1/4 teaspoon ground black pepper
1/4 cup chopped pecans

Cream together the butter, sugar, molasses, and bourbon in a bowl using an electric mixer on medium speed until smooth and well blended, scraping down sides of bowl as necessary. Mix flour, salt, ginger, cinnamon, nutmeg, pepper and chopped pecans in another bowl. Add to the butter mixture and mix well. Add a bit of extra flour if the dough is not stiff enough to hold its shape. Drop dough by 1-teaspoon portions, 3 inches apart, onto parchment-lined baking sheets. Bake cookies in a 300 degree oven for about 20 minutes or until slightly crispy. (To ensure perfectly round snaps, take the cookies out of the oven halfway through the baking process and use a spatula to push in the edges and give the cookies a nice round shape.) Remove from the oven, let sit for a minute or two, and use a wide spatula to transfer warm cookies to racks to cool. Dust half of each snap with powdered sugar. Serve with crème brûlée and enjoy.

Elijah Craig Ice Cream

Elijah Craig, a Baptist preacher from Kentucky credited with the founding of Georgetown College, is most often recognized for his contribution to the bourbon industry in Kentucky. A shrewd businessman as well, Craig started a distillery in Bourbon County in the late 1700s. It was here that corn whiskey would first be aged in charred, new oak barrels that resulted in the rich amber spirit known as bourbon. Medium-tawny brown in color, and with aromas of vanilla and spice with honey and nutmeg notes, the bourbon that bears his name today figures prominently in a Bourbon County favorite known as Elijah Craig ice cream. Based on a frozen-custard recipe, this rich and silky concoction relies on the down-to-earth goodness of cinnamon to bring out the natural sweetness of cream and bourbon.

2 cups whole milk
1 cup granulated sugar
3 large eggs
3 tablespoons all-purpose flour
2 teaspoons ground cinnamon
1 teaspoon vanilla extract
1/4 teaspoon salt
1/4 cup bourbon
2 cups heavy cream

Whisk together the milk, sugar, eggs, flour, cinnamon, vanilla extract and salt in a saucepan over medium-low heat. Cook until the mixture thickens, stirring often. Remove from the heat, add the bourbon, mix well and allow to cool. Whip the cream in a large bowl until soft peaks form. Once the custard mixture has cooled completely, fold it into the whipped cream. If there are lumps in the custard, you may want to purée the mixture in a blender before adding to the whipped cream. Transfer to an electric ice cream maker and follow the manufacturer's instructions for making ice cream.

Elderberry Sherbet

Although the elderberry was well known to previous generations, it is often overlooked today as a source of tasty recipes and household remedies. Such neglect is unfortunate, however, since these bushes grow wild in many parts of the country. Often referred to as the Englishman's grape, the elderberry flowers and berries have been used in a variety of ways in Bluegrass kitchens for many years. When hunting fresh elderberries, seek the blue variety in flat clusters and not the red variety in domed clusters, as the latter are distasteful and sometimes poisonous.

6 cups elderberries
1 cup granulated sugar
1/2 cup water
1/4 cup fresh lemon juice
2 cups heavy cream
2 egg whites
1/4 teaspoon salt

Place the berries in a saucepan with the sugar, water and lemon juice. Cover and gently simmer over low heat for about 45 minutes, or until the berries have started to break down. Let cool and strain the berries through a sieve, discarding the pulp. About 2 cups of rich elderberry syrup should remain. Taste it, and add more sugar if required. Whip the cream until stiff peaks form. Whip the egg whites in a separate bowl until they are stiff and add the salt. Fold the cream into the egg whites and gently add the elderberry syrup, until the mixture has taken on a nice purple color. Pour the mixture into an electric ice cream maker and follow the manufacturer's instructions.

Appalachian Pound Cake

Made from a pound of butter, a pound of sugar, a pound of eggs, and a pound of flour, traditional American pound cake has always been a favorite across the South. In the eastern part of the state, the Bluegrass flavors of bourbon and ground spicebush berries, also known as poor man's cloves, often find their ways into a rich batter enhanced with southern staples like brown sugar and buttermilk. The result is a buttery, sweet delight that can be enjoyed any time of the day.

3 cups cake flour
1/2 teaspoon baking soda
1 teaspoon baking powder
1/2 teaspoon salt
1 teaspoon ground
   spicebush berries
2 cups butter, softened
1 cup granulated sugar
1 cup light brown sugar
6 large eggs
2 teaspoons vanilla extract
1/2 cup buttermilk
1/2 cup bourbon

Preheat the oven to 350 degrees. Sift the flour, baking soda and baking powder into a large mixing bowl. Stir in salt and spicebush. Cream together the butter and sugars using an electric mixer until light and fluffy. Continue mixing and add the eggs, one at a time, until well incorporated. Add the flour mixture and begin mixing on very low speed. Add the vanilla extract, buttermilk and bourbon and gradually bring up to high speed. Mix only until the batter is smooth and free of lumps. Grease a very large cast-iron skillet or 2 loaf pans and spoon in the batter. Gently tap the pan on a counter or table top several times to bring any air bubbles to the surface. Bake 1 hour to 1 hour and 15 minutes, until a wooden toothpick inserted the center of the cake comes out clean. Allow the cake to cool for 15 minutes in the pan, and then gently remove it. Finish cooling on a baking rack. This cake can be enjoyed alone or served dusted with powdered sugar alongside ice cream and sweetened whipped cream.

Chocolate Bourbon Gingerbread

Baking gingerbread perfumes a kitchen like no other food known to man. Although it manages to make a comeback as the Christmas holidays approach, gingerbread must sadly be considered one of those old-fashioned standards that have fallen out of favor in American kitchens. But, add a bit of good Kentucky bourbon and the decadent flavor of chocolate, and this sure-fire recipe is certain to become a favorite dessert in your Bluegrass repertoire. Serve it with warm chocolate sauce and hand-whipped cream, and you'll wonder why you never made this wonderful treat before.

1/2 cup unsalted butter, softened
1/2 cup dark brown sugar
1/2 cup molasses
2 large eggs
1 1/2 cups cake flour
1/4 cup cocoa powder
1/2 teaspoon baking soda
1/2 teaspoon kosher salt
1/4 teaspoon baking powder
1 tablespoon ground ginger
1 teaspoon ground cinnamon
2 tablespoons prepared
   yellow mustard
1 teaspoon vanilla extract
1/2 cup buttermilk
1/4 cup bourbon
Powdered sugar and cocoa
   for dusting

Preheat oven to 350 degrees. Cream together the butter and brown sugar in a mixing bowl until light and fluffy. Add the molasses and continue mixing. Once the molasses has been incorporated, add the eggs, one at a time, and beat well. Mix the dry ingredients and add to the butter-and-egg mixture. Add the mustard, vanilla extract, buttermilk and bourbon and mix well. Be careful not to over mix as this will produce a tough cake and many air tunnels. Pour the batter into miniature cake pans, a large charlotte or soufflé pan that has been buttered and dusted with flour. Bake in the oven for 20 minutes or until a wooden pick inserted in the center comes out clean. Let cool for 10 minutes and turn the cake upside down out of the pan onto a serving plate. Dust with a mixture of powdered sugar and cocoa and enjoy.

Use any remaining powdered sugar and cocoa and add to cream and hand mix until combined and fluffy. Top the gingerbread with the flavored cream.

Blackberry Jam Cake

For many Kentuckians, summer evokes memories of baggy clothes and blackberry picking among the brambles in rural parts of the state. But the toil can be very rewarding, especially months later when jars of blackberry preserves and jams emerge from the pantry and recall the warm sun and pleasant days of summer. Many Bluegrass bakers prefer to use their prized blackberry jam in an old-fashioned American favorite known as blackberry jam cake, a rich spice cake topped off with a decadent caramel icing that is often served at Christmas time.

1 cup unsalted butter, softened
2 cups brown sugar
4 large eggs, beaten
1 cup seedless blackberry jam
3 cups cake flour
1 teaspoon baking soda
1/2 teaspoon baking powder
1 teaspoon allspice
1 teaspoon ground cinnamon
1/2 teaspoon salt
1 cup buttermilk
1 cup cream cheese, softened
1 cup light brown sugar
1 cup powdered sugar
2 tablespoons bourbon

Preheat oven to 350 degrees. Cream butter and sugar in a mixing bowl until light and fluffy. Add eggs, one at a time, beating well after each addition. Add jam and mix well. Sift together flour, baking soda, baking powder, allspice, cinnamon and salt. Add to the creamed butter and eggs, alternately with the buttermilk, mixing well after each addition. Divide the mixture evenly and spoon into three greased-and-floured 9-inch cake pans. Bake 20-30 minutes or until a pick inserted in the center comes out clean. Let cakes cool in the pans for 10 minutes and then remove to wire racks to cool completely. Layer and ice the cake with a frosting made by beating softened cream cheese with brown sugar, powdered sugar and bourbon.

Wild Turkey Pavers with Black Walnuts

Said to be America's best-selling, super-premium bourbon, Wild Turkey Bourbon is carefully crafted in Lawrenceburg under the watchful eye of Master Distiller Jimmy Russell. Aging in charred new oak barrels imbues the high-proof whiskey with an amber sheen and rich honey notes of caramel and vanilla that match well with chocolate. This chocolaty recipe for truffle-like confections that resemble the cobblestones or pavers in the streets of French villages also features black walnuts and cinnamon for a festive flavor. For a real Bluegrass treat, use chocolate from Jamieson's in Mt. Sterling.

1 cup heavy cream
8 ounces Jamieson's
  Mellow Dark Chocolate
2 cups semisweet chocolate chips
1/2 teaspoon cinnamon
1/2 teaspoon vanilla extract
1/4 teaspoon salt
1 cup black walnut pieces, chopped

Heat the cream in a saucepan until it barely reaches the boiling point, being careful not to bring it to a boil. Chop the Jamieson's chocolates into small pieces and place along with the chocolate chips in a large bowl. Pour the hot cream over it, let it sit for 1-2 minutes and whisk together until all the chocolate has melted. Add the cinnamon, vanilla extract and salt and continue mixing until the mixture is smooth and satiny. Add the nuts and spread the chocolate in a buttered 9x13-inch cake pan. Refrigerate for 2 or 3 hours or until the chocolate has become firm. Run a sharp knife around the edges of the pan to loosen the chocolate and turn the pan upside down on a cutting surface to dislodge. Use a cleaver or knife to cut the block into 1/2-inch squares or pavers and, if desired, toss each one in cocoa powder to coat.

Modjeskas

The year is 1883, and all eyes are turned to Louisville, Kentucky, where the doors have recently opened for the Great Southern Exposition. Helena Modjeska, the famed Polish actress, is performing the lead role in Ibsen's world premier of *A Doll's House* at McCauley's Theater. Anton Busath, a local confectioner who has just seen the production, decides to rename a delicious marshmallow specialty known as the caramel biscuit to honor the renowned stage performer. Since then, Modjeskas have delighted many a sweet tooth across the Bluegrass with their billowy marshmallow centers draped in creamy caramel. To make both the caramel and marshmallows from scratch can be a time-consuming endeavor, but the end results are well worth the effort.

Marshmallows

2 cups granulated sugar
1/2 cup light corn syrup
1/2 cup hot water
1/4 teaspoon salt
3 1/2 envelopes unflavored gelatin
1/2 cup cold water
2 large egg whites
1 teaspoon vanilla extract
1 cup powdered sugar

Combine sugar, butter, syrup, 1 cup of cream and salt in a heavy 4-quart saucepan over medium heat. Heat the remaining cream in a separate pan. Bring the sugar-cream-butter mixture to a boil, stirring constantly and wiping down the sides of the pan with a wet cloth to dissolve any remaining sugar crystals. When a rolling boil begins, slowly stir in the remaining cream, careful not to let the boiling stop. Cook over medium heat, stirring as necessary to prevent scorching until a thermometer registers about 235 degrees. Remove from heat and stir in vanilla extract and bourbon. Allow cooked caramel to cool for 10 minutes before starting to dip. Dip each marshmallow into caramel, then turn it over with a fork to coat completely and lift out. Let excess caramel drip off and place each piece on waxed paper to cool. When set, wrap each piece individually in waxed paper.

Combine granulated sugar, corn syrup, hot water, and salt in a large, heavy saucepan and cook over low heat, stirring with a wooden spoon, until sugar is dissolved. Increase heat to moderate and boil for 10-12 minutes, without stirring, until a candy thermometer registers 240 degrees. While the syrup is cooking, sprinkle gelatin over cold water in a large bowl. Stir and allow it to soften. Remove pan from heat and pour sugar mixture over gelatin mixture, stirring until gelatin is completely dissolved. Beat with an electric mixer on high speed until white, thick, and tripled in volume. Beat the egg whites in a separate large bowl with cleaned beaters until stiff peaks form. Beat whites and vanilla into sugar mixture until just combined. Pour mixture into a 9x13-inch baking pan that has been greased and dusted with powdered sugar. Sift 1/4 cup sugar over the top. Chill uncovered, for at least 3 hours, until firm.

Apple Stack Cakes with Bourbon Whipped Cream

Stack cakes have been said to be the most "mountain" of all Bluegrass desserts. Legend has it that early Kentucky pioneer James Harrod, the founder of Harrodsburg, brought the recipe for this typical Appalachian cake with him when he traveled the Wilderness Road to Kentucky. Since then it has been a specialty among mountain folk in the eastern part of the state, where it was a favorite pioneer wedding cake. Since wedding cakes were often very expensive, guests invited to potluck style wedding parties often brought layers of cake to donate to the bride's family. They would in turn stack the cakes with layers of dried apples cooked with sugar and spices, and the height of the cake would often indicate the bride's popularity.

2 cups granulated sugar
1 cup butter, softened
2 large eggs
6 cups all-purpose flour
3 teaspoons baking powder
1 teaspoon baking soda
1/2 teaspoon salt
1 cup buttermilk
1 tablespoon vanilla extract

Preheat oven to 400 degrees. Cream the granulated sugar and butter in a large bowl. Add eggs, one at a time, beating well after each addition. Sift flour with baking powder, soda and salt. Add flour to butter mixture, alternating with buttermilk and vanilla extract and mix until well incorporated. Divide dough into eight equal parts. If baking on cookie sheets, roll the dough into rounds on a well-floured surface or pat into well-greased 9-inch pans. It is important that the rounds be uniform in size. Bake for 10-15 minutes until browned and cool on wire racks. Once the layers have cooled, spread each with apple filling and layer in a 9-inch pan.

Filling

16 ounces dried apples
1 cup light brown sugar
1 teaspoon ground cinnamon
1/4 teaspoon ground cloves
1/4 teaspoon ground allspice

Cook apples with the sugar and spices in enough water to cover until soft. Once cooked, purée and cool before spreading between layers.

For a decadent garnish, whip 2 cups heavy cream with 1/2 cup powdered sugar and 2 tablespoons bourbon.

Bourbon Chocolate Scones

Although these chocolate treats are perfect for an afternoon tea, they can also be enjoyed at breakfast or as a light dessert. Chunks of Kentucky-made chocolate add an extra bit of sweetness to a rich dough flavored with cocoa and bourbon.

1 cup heavy whipping cream
1/2 cup bourbon
2 large eggs, lightly beaten
1 tablespoon vanilla extract
3 cups all-purpose flour
1/2 cup Dutch-processed
  unsweetened cocoa powder
1 1/2 cups granulated sugar
1/4 cup powdered sugar
3 teaspoons baking powder
1 teaspoon salt
1 cup unsalted butter,
  cold and cut into small pieces
1 cup semisweet chocolate pieces
1 large egg, well beaten
1 tablespoon heavy cream
Powdered sugar for dusting
Whipped cream or honey butter

Preheat oven to 375 degrees. Whisk together the whipping cream, bourbon, egg, and vanilla extract in a small bowl and set aside. Sift together flour, cocoa powder, sugars, baking powder and salt in a separate bowl. Use a pastry blender or your hands to cut the butter into the flour mixture until it resembles cornmeal. Carefully add the cream mixture and chocolate pieces to the flour mixture to form a soft dough. You may need to add extra bourbon or flour if the dough is too dry or sticky. Transfer the dough to a lightly floured board, gently knead and shape the dough into a 1-inch-thick circle. Cut the dough into triangles or rounds and place on a parchment-lined baking sheet. Bake for 15 minutes or until firm. A toothpick inserted into the center of a scone should come out clean. Cool on a wire rack, dust with powdered sugar and serve with sweetened whipped cream or honey butter.

Drinks

Raspberry Bourbon Shrub
Pages 168 & 169

Mint Julep

Nothing can bring out a good southern drawl like a Mint Julep. It has been a symbol of Bluegrass gentility since the 1700s, and it is the only drink that comes to mind when talking about the Kentucky Derby. Take a sultry summer's day and a group of good friends on a front porch, and you've got the perfect fixings for an afternoon get-together. Produced by Louisville-based Brown-Forman Corporation since 1923, Early Times Kentucky Whisky is a Bluegrass favorite, and the Early Times Mint Julep was named the official drink of the Kentucky Derby in 1987. Nowadays, nearly 90,000 of the traditional highballs are enjoyed every year at the Run for the Roses at Churchill Downs. This recipe uses Early Times in my version of the quintessential Kentucky cocktail.

4 large sprigs of fresh mint
2 teaspoons powdered sugar
2 ounces Early Times
1/2 cup crushed ice
Soda water

In a chilled silver tumbler or highball glass, muddle 3 sprigs of the mint with the powdered sugar until the mint leaves are bruised. Add the bourbon and stir until the sugar is dissolved. Add the ice, top off with soda water and stir to mix well. Garnish with the remaining mint sprig (dusted with powdered sugar if you like) and enjoy.

2 ounces bourbon
1 ounce fresh lemon juice
1 teaspoon powdered sugar
1 twist lemon peel

In a cocktail shaker half filled with crushed ice, shake the bourbon, lemon juice and sugar until well blended. Pour in a highball or martini glass, garnish with the lemon twist and enjoy.

Bourbon Sling

Invented at the Raffles Hotel in Singapore sometime in the early 1900s, the Singapore Sling with its gin, cherry brandy and exotic fruit is perhaps the most famous of all the *sling* drinks. Long before that, however, and well before the advent of the modern cocktail, slings counted as one of the most popular types of alcoholic beverages in this country. Barkeeps would *sling* a good dram of liquor together with water and sugar for a potent and flavorful beverage.

2 ounces Rain vodka
5 ounces strong iced tea
1 teaspoon honey
Ice

For one serving, add the vodka, iced tea and honey to a cocktail mixer half-filled with crushed ice. Shake well and strain over ice cubes in a frosted high ball glass.

Ice Pick

Iced teas and sweet teas, without a doubt, figure among the most prominent of all southern beverages, and they can be found on dinner tables at any time of the year, not just in the summer. Add a shot of vodka, and you've got a refreshing drink known as an ice pick. This simple preparation calls for Rain vodka, an award-winning Kentucky spirit handmade from scratch in small batches at Buffalo Trace Distillery in Frankfort. Distilled exclusively from 100 percent organic white corn, Rain vodka undergoes an extensive 20-day production technique that includes cold-water sweet mash fermentation, seven distinct distillations and a polishing stage that adds pure limestone water.

Old-Fashioned

One of Kentucky's most famed contributions to the world of cocktails, the Old-Fashioned first came into being in the 1880s at the Pendennis Club in downtown Louisville. Invented by a bartender at that club, the Old-Fashioned was popularized by Colonel James E. Pepper, a club member and bourbon distiller, who eventually took the recipe to the Waldorf-Astoria Hotel bar in New York City. The old Pepper family distillery now produces hand-crafted Woodford Reserve bourbon, which is the logical choice for this time-honored Bluegrass favorite.

1/2 teaspoon extra-fine sugar
2 dashes Angostura bitters
1 piece lemon peel
2 ounces bourbon
   (such as Woodford Reserve)
2-3 ice cubes

In a whiskey tumbler, muddle together the sugar, bitters and lemon peel until the lemon peel has started to break up. Add a few drops of water to help dissolve the sugar and mix well. Add the bourbon and ice cubes, stir around a bit and enjoy. Although many bartenders top the cocktail off with a splash of soda and add an orange slice and maraschino cherry to the muddle, this deviates from the original recipe and most likely arose during Prohibition as a way to cover the taste of low-quality alcohol. For an eye-catching garnish, use a sharp paring knife to strip the peel from a lemon in one long piece and coil it on top of the drink.

Kentucky Cobbler

2 ounces bourbon
3 ounces Ale-8-One
1 maraschino cherry
1 orange slice
1 lemon slice

In a highball glass, add crushed ice until the glass is almost full. Add the bourbon and Ale-8-One and stir well. Skewer the cherry, orange and lemon slices on a toothpick and garnish.

In the world of recipes, most people think of a fruit dessert when the word cobbler is mentioned, however, it can also refer to a tall iced drink made with wine or liquor and fruit. In many respects, most bourbon old fashioneds that people are served in bars today would more accurately be called cobblers due to addition of fruit and iced soda water. This Kentucky classic combines two Bluegrass favorites – bourbon and Ale-8-One – to make a slightly sweet, refreshing highball.

Lilies

Every year on the first Saturday in May, the eyes of the world turn to the track at Churchill Downs in Louisville for the famed Run for the Roses, "the most exciting two minutes in sports." However, the Friday before also sees a great deal of excitement when fillies gather for the Run for the Lilies at the Kentucky Oaks. This drink is meant to honor that special day with a celebratory combination of California sparkling wine and Kentucky bourbon laced with the inviting flavors of ginger and orange. A pineapple-shaped garnish made from lemon peel and mint recalls the traditional American symbol for hospitality.

1/2 ounce Old Forester Bourbon
1/2 ounce Canton Ginger liqueur
1/2 ounce Cointreau
3 ounces Korbel California Champagne
Lemons and mint sprigs for garnish

Pour the bourbon, ginger liqueur and Cointreau in a champagne flute and top off with sparkling wine. To prepare the garnish, slice off two large oval discs of lemon peel with a sharp knife and place them together with the yellow sides facing out; this will form the body of the pineapple. Use a very sharp knife to make a 1/4-inch vertical slit at the bottom through both pieces of peel and use this to affix the pineapple garnish to the rim of the glass. Take a sprig of mint and place it between the two pieces of peel at the top of the pineapple and press together to hold the mint sprig; this will form the frond of the pineapple.

Race Day Spritzer

Mainers have their Moxie, Texans have their Dr. Pepper, and folks in the Bluegrass have their Ale-8-One. Bottled in Winchester since 1926, the formula for this unique Kentucky soft drink developed by G.L. Wainscott is still a closely guarded family secret that traces its origins to northern Europe. Wainscott supposedly liked the ginger-based soft drinks he sampled during his many travels there and brought the inspiration back for a new soft drink. In need of a name for the new beverage, he sponsored one of the country's first "name-the-product" contests, and "A Late One" was chosen. The drink's logo, Ale-8-One, was adopted as a sort of pun for "the latest thing" in soft drinks. Paired with Broad Run Vineyard's fruity, spicy Gewurtztraminer, it makes a refreshing summertime drink perfect for picnics or a day at the track.

For each serving:

4 ounces Ale-8-One
4 ounces dry white wine
1/2 teaspoon confectioners' sugar
Lemon slices for garnish
1/2 cup crushed ice

Refrigerate the Ale-8-One and wine until well chilled. Combine the Ale-8-One, wine, confectioners' sugar and ice in a cocktail pitcher and give it a good stir. Quickly strain so the ice doesn't have a chance to melt and water down the drink. Pour the mixture into a chilled wine glass for service. Garnish with slices of lemon and enjoy. For an added treat, make an extra fruity spritzer by adding a half cup of gently mashed raspberries or sliced fresh strawberries to the wine glass right before serving.

Raspberry Bourbon Shrub

4 cups fresh or frozen raspberries
2 cups apple cider vinegar
2 cups granulated sugar
Sparkling water
Bourbon

Raspberry shrub was one of the most popular drinks in the America of the 1800s and owes much of its popularity to the Temperance Movement, which promoted it as an alternative to hard spirits and beer. The word *shrub* comes from the old Arabic word meaning *drink* and amounted to a tart, fruit-based syrup that would be cut with cold water and sometimes alcohol to produce a refreshing summertime beverage. In Kentucky, as in most parts of the country, shrubs were also known as *vinegars*, no doubt because vinegar was a key ingredient used to macerate the fruit, and they could be made from a wide variety of fruits and berries. Not surprising, Kentuckians often added bourbon whiskey to their shrubs for a more potent concoction.

Simmer the raspberries and vinegar in a large saucepan for 20 minutes or until the berries have started to break down. Transfer the mixture to a blender and purée. Once the mixture has cooled slightly, strain it through a sieve to remove all the seeds and pulp. There should be at least 3 cups of juice, if not, you'll have to add some water to make up the difference. Transfer to a saucepan with the sugar and simmer for 20-30 minutes until the sugar is dissolved and the syrup is thick and ruby red. For each shrub, you will need to mix together 1 part syrup with 2 parts sparkling water and a splash of bourbon.

1 teaspoon extra fine sugar
1 pinch salt
1/4 cup crushed ice
3-4 dashes Peychaud® bitters
1 1/2 ounces **Basil Hayden's
   Kentucky Bourbon Whiskey**
1 dash **Absinthe or Pernod**
1 dash soda water
1 twist lemon peel

Chill an old-fashioned glass in the freezer. Combine the sugar and salt with the ice, Absinthe and bitters in a cocktail shaker. Add the bourbon and shake well. Pour into a chilled glass, top off with soda water and garnish with lemon peel.

Bourbon Sazerac

Said to be America's first cocktail, the Sazerac traces its roots back to early 19th-century New Orleans when a West Indian apothecary used a proprietary blend of bitters to flavor a cognac-based drink for his customers. The Sazerac name derives from the brand of cognac originally used in the drink, however with the passage of time, rye whiskey evolved as the main ingredient and a dash of anise-flavored liquor was added. This Bluegrass version of the recipe uses Basil Hayden's Kentucky Bourbon Whiskey from Buffalo Trace Distillery because of its high rye content. This remarkable bourbon dates back to 1796, when Basil Hayden himself was a master distiller. Born and raised in Maryland, he learned to make whiskey from rye and carried the tradition to Kentucky, where he began making whiskey from a base of corn, but with a higher percentage of rye than other distillers, resulting in a smooth, mild bourbon.

For each toddy:

1 shot bourbon
2 tablespoons honey
1 tablespoon fresh lemon juice
1 orange slice
1/2 cup boiling water

Stir together the bourbon, honey and lemon juice in a heavy mug until the honey has dissolved. Add the orange slice and pour in the boiling water and stir.

Hot Bourbon Toddies

A good hot toddy has been said to loosen the spirit and warm the body. They can be made with Scotch or brandy, however, the natural caramel and vanilla flavors of good bourbon make it the best choice for hot toddies. This recipe works especially well with a good drinking bourbon like Evan Williams. Widely considered "Kentucky's first distiller," Williams arrived in Louisville in 1783 and set up a small distillery along the Ohio River at the foot of what is now Fifth Street. The bourbon that bears his name today is bottled at Heaven Hill Distilleries.

Mulled Cider with Bourbon

Mulled cider, like mulled wine or hot cocoa, has become a cold-weather tradition in many homes. It is a warm, comforting drink that is easy to prepare. Good Kentucky bourbon and aromatic spice berries added to this traditional recipe make it a sure-to-please Bluegrass drink.

6 cups apple cider
1 large orange, sliced
1 lemon, sliced
2-3 cinnamon sticks
1 tablespoon spicebush berries
1 cup bourbon

Pour the apple cider into a large pot or saucepan set over low heat. Add the sliced orange and lemon, cinnamon sticks and allspice berries and let simmer for half an hour. Add the bourbon and simmer for another 5 minutes. Ladle into large mugs to serve, and enjoy.

1 cup whole milk

1 ounce Jamieson's Robust Dark
   Chocolate, broken into pieces

1 tablespoon honey

1 pinch salt

1 shot bourbon

Whipped cream and ground
   cinnamon for garnish

Heat the milk in a saucepan, careful to
keep it from boiling. Once heated, pour
it into a blender with the chocolate,
honey, salt and bourbon, and blend until
the chocolate has dissolved completely.
Pour into a warmed mug and enjoy
with a garnish of fresh whipped cream
and ground cinnamon.

Bluegrass Hot Chocolate

Nothing is more comforting on
a cold winter's day than a steaming
mug of hot chocolate. When
it's made with West African chocolate imported by a Bluegrass
chocolatier, and then spiked with a
shot of good Kentucky bourbon,
it can only get better. David and
Susan Jamieson founded their
company in 1998 to introduce
chocolate from Ghana to residents
of the Bluegrass, and since then
Jamieson's has become a division
of the Ruth Hunt Candy Company.

List of Kentucky Growers and Producers

A Taste of Kentucky
11800 Shelbyville Road, Suite 4
Louisville, Kentucky 40243
800-444-0552

Abbey of Gethsemani
3642 Monks Road
Trappist, Kentucky 40051
502-549-3117

Acres of Land Winery
2285 Barnes Mill Road
Richmond, Kentucky 40475
859-328-3000

Ale-8-One Bottling Company, Inc.
25 Carol Road
Winchester, Kentucky 40391
859-744-3484

Alltech's Lexington Brewing Company
401 Cross Street
Lexington, Kentucky 40508
859-887-3406

Barker's Blackberry Hill Winery
16629 Mt. Zion-Verona Road
Crittenden, Kentucky 41030
859-428-0377

Barton Brands
1 Barton Road
Bardstown, Kentucky 40004
502-348-3991

Bravard Vineyards & Winery
15000 Overton Road
Hopkinsville, Kentucky 42240
270-269-2583

Broad Run Vineyards
10601 Broad Run Road
Louisville, Kentucky 40299
502-231-0372

Broadbent Hams
6321 Hopkinsville Road
Cadiz, Kentucky 42211
800-841-2202

Bubba Sue's Shrimp Company
Duntreath Farm
4954 Paris Pike
Lexington, Kentucky 40511
859-299-2254

Buffalo Trace Distillery
1001 Wilkinson Boulevard
Frankfort, Kentucky 40601
800-654-8471

Capriole Farms
P.O. Box 117
10329 Newcut Road
Greenville, Indiana 47124
812-923-9408

Century House Winery & Vineyard
Lewisburg, Kentucky 42256
270-221-0331

Chateau du Vieux Corbeau Winery
471 Stanford Road
Danville, Kentucky 40422
859-236-1808

Chrisman Mill Vineyards & Winery
2385 Chrisman Mill Road
Nicholasville, Kentucky 40356
859-881-5007

Equus Run Vineyards
1280 Moores Mill Road
Midway, Kentucky 40347
859-846-WINE

Father's Country Hams, Inc.
Gatton Farms
P.O. Box 99
Bremen, Kentucky 42325
877-525-4267

Finchville Farms
P.O. Box 56
Finchville, Kentucky 40022
800-678-1521

Four Roses Distillery
1224 Bonds Hill Road
Lawrenceburg, Kentucky 40342
502-839-3436

Happy Balls!
Old Louisville Candy Co.
1390 South Third Street
Louiville, Kentucky 40208
502-637-2227

Harper's Country Hams
P.O. Box 122
2955 Highway 51 North
Clinton, Kentucky 42031
888-HAR-PERS

Heaven Hill Distilleries
P.O. Box 787
1311 Gilkey Run Road
Bardstown, Kentucky 40004
502-337-1000

Heritage Pointe Vineyards
Route 2, Box 114
Vanceburg, Kentucky 41179
606-798-1205

Highland Winery
193 Seco Drive
Seco, Kentucky 41849
606-855-7968

Huber's Orchard & Winery
19816 Huber Road
Starlight, Indiana 47106
812-923-9463

In Town Winery
414 Baxter Avenue
Louisville, Kentucky 40204
502-540-5650

Integration Acres Ltd.
160 Cherry Ridge Road
Albany, Ohio 45710
740-698-6060

Jamieson's Chocolates
550 North Maysville Road
Mt. Sterling, Kentucky 40353
800-927-0302

Keene's Hams
8 Old Bloomfield Pike
Bardstown, Kentucky 40004
877-348-3594

Kenny's Farmhouse Cheese
2033 Thomerson Park Road
Austin, Kentucky 42123
888-571-4029

Kentucky Barrels, LLC
P.O. Box 1684
Danville, Kentucky 40423
606-346-9375

Kentucky Bourbon Distillers, Ltd.
1869 Loretto Road, P.O. Box 785
Bardstown, Kentucky 40004
502-348-0081

Kentucky Cattlemen's Association
176 Pasadena Drive
Lexington, Kentucky 40503
859-278-0899

Kinder Caviar
P.O. Box 61
Perry Park, Kentucky 40363
502-484-2272

La Ferme du Cerf Winery
1000 Perkins Road
Dry Ridge, Kentucky 41053
859-428-5655

Laura's Lean Beef Company
2285 Executive Drive, Suite 200
Lexington, Kentucky 40505
859-299-7707

Lost Heritage Vineyards
3748 Ridgewood Court
Alexandria, Kentucky 41001
859-635-2949

Lover's Leap Vineyard & Winery
129 Lover's Leap
Lawrenceburg, Kentucky 40342
502-839-7952

Maker's Mark Distillery, Inc.
3350 Burks Spring Road
Loretto, Kentucky 40037
502-459-7884

Mclain and Kyne Distillery Limited
1003 Alta Vista Road
Louisville Kentucky 40205
502-896-8003

Newsom's Country Hams
208 East Main Street
Princeton, Kentucky 42445
270-365-2482

Old Rip Van Winkle Distillery
2843 Brownsboro Road
Louisville, Kentucky 40206
502-897-9113

Paris, Bourbon County Farmers Market &
Market Store
720 High Street
Paris, Kentucky 40361
859-987-6614

Penn's Country Hams
P.O. Box 88
Mansville, Kentucky 42758
800-883-6984

Poultry in Motion
1621 Tatum Ridge
Willisburg, Kentucky 40078
859-375-2690

Ruth Hunt Candies
550 North Maysville Road
Mt. Sterling, Kentucky 40353
800-927-0302

Rolling Hills Vineyard & Winery
2385 Kelly Shop Road
Springfield, Kentucky 40069
859-262-6154

Shuckman's Fish Company & Smokery
3001 West Main Street
Louisville, Kentucky 40212
502-775-6478

Smith-Berry Winery
P O Box 44 (Hwy 202)
New Castle, Kentucky 40050
502-845-7091

Sour Mash Bourbon Bread Company
1370 Belmar Drive
Louisville, Kentucky 40213
502-643-2969

Springhill Winery & Plantation B&B
3205 Springfield Road
Bloomfield, Kentucky 40008
502-252-9463

StoneBrook Winery
6570 Vineyard Lane
Melbourne, Kentucky 41059
859-635-4590

Stovers Family Vineyard
200 Holly Branch Run
Magnolia, Kentucky 42757
270-324-2455

Talon Winery & Vineyards
7086 Tates Creek Road
Lexington, Kentucky 40515
859-971-3214

The Old Pogue Distillery
100 Lebanon Avenue
Campbellsville, Kentucky 42718
317-697-5039

The Wild Turkey Distillery
US Route 62
Lawrenceburg, Kentucky 40342
502-839-4544

Effective July 2008 some cities in the 270 area code will change to a 364 area code.

WIDMER HOUSE

Index

Salads

Sides

Soups

Sweets

As a young child, best-selling author David Dominé always found himself surrounded by female relatives in the kitchen, and since that time, he has had an unending fascination with food and kitchen culture. As an adult foodie, extended stays in countries as diverse as the Philippines, Austria, Mexico, Spain, Italy and Germany afforded him excellent opportunities to gain first-hand knowledge of world cuisine. He seized upon every opportunity to experience the culinary arts, and when he returned to this country, he did so with a newfound appreciation for American food and culture.

David Dominé

Kentucky became his home in 1993, and he was immediately struck by the distinct culinary tradition that forms the Bluegrass food experience. For years, he has explored remote corners of the commonwealth in search of the perfect meal, all the while gaining an increased fondness for his adopted state and its colorful characters.

David contributes pieces to a wide variety of publications, but many of his food articles can be read in *Kentucky Monthly* magazine, where he is senior correspondent, and *Arts Across Kentucky*, where he writes a regular column called *Edible Art*. He is the successful author of two books, *Ghosts of Old Louisville* and *Phantoms of Old Louisville*, both published by McClanahan Publishing House.